Hill Walkers Kerry

36 Walking Routes in the Dingle and Iveragh Peninsulas

David Herman

SHANKSMARE PUBLICATIONS

The mist soon penetrated our clothes and we began to experience all the inconvenience of wet and cold, when the guide, stopping suddenly, took off his coat, turned it inside out, and again deliberately put it on. We marvelled very much at this extraordinary proceeding.[...] At last, being pressed for an explanation, he acknowleged that he was totally ignorant of our situation, and had turned his coat as a charm of potent influence to enable a lost man to recover his way. The intelligence was unwelcome: the day was fast approaching to a close, and there was a danger of our taking the very opposite course to that which ought to be followed.

A description of a climb on Mangerton from *'Illustrations of the Scenery of Killarney and the surrounding Country'* (1812) by Isaac Weld.

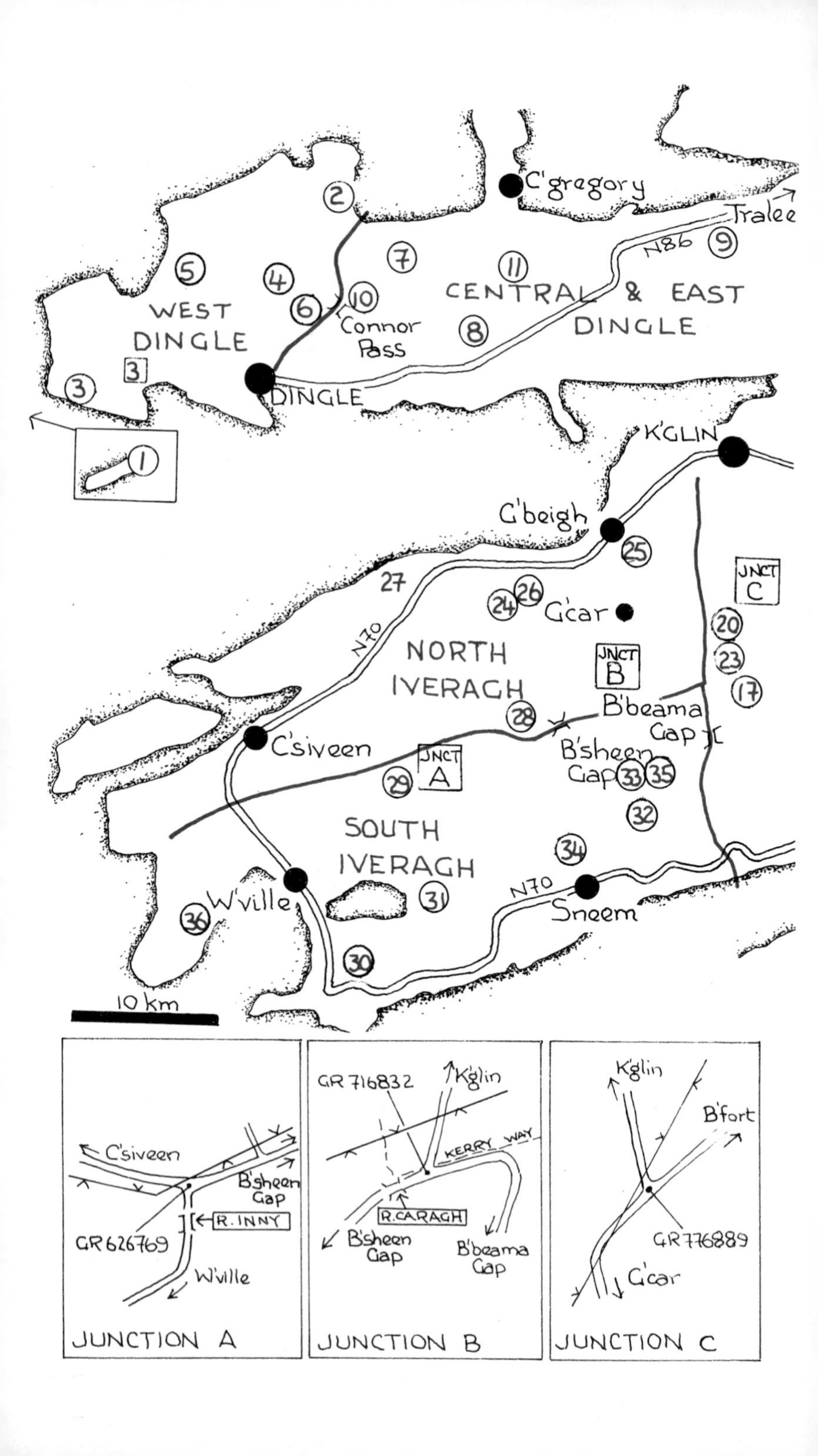

C'gregory
Tralee
N86
CENTRAL & EAST DINGLE
WEST DINGLE
Connor Pass
DINGLE
K'GLIN
C'beigh
27
N70
G'car
JNCT C
NORTH IVERAGH
JNCT B
B'beama Gap
C'siveen
JNCT A
B'sheen Gap
SOUTH IVERAGH
W'ville
N70
Sneem
10 km
C'siveen
B'sheen Gap
R. INNY
GR 626769
W'ville
JUNCTION A
GR 716832
K'glin
KERRY WAY
R. CARAGH
B'sheen Gap
B'beama Gap
JUNCTION B
K'glin
B'fort
GR 776889
G'car
JUNCTION C

CONTENTS

A Quick Look Around p4; How to Use this Book p4; Getting to Kerry p5: Getting Around Kerry p5; Accommodation p7; Maps p7; Long Distance Paths p8; A Few Route Selections p8 Safety p9; What to Carry with you p9; Rights of Way and Good Conduct p10; They're your Mountains - Get Involved! p10; Useful Contacts p11.

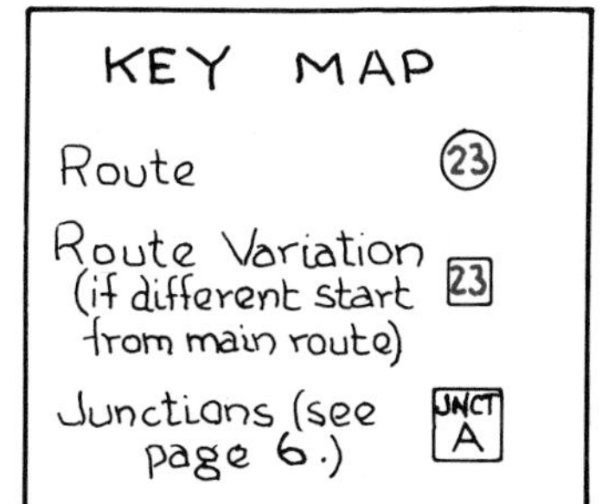

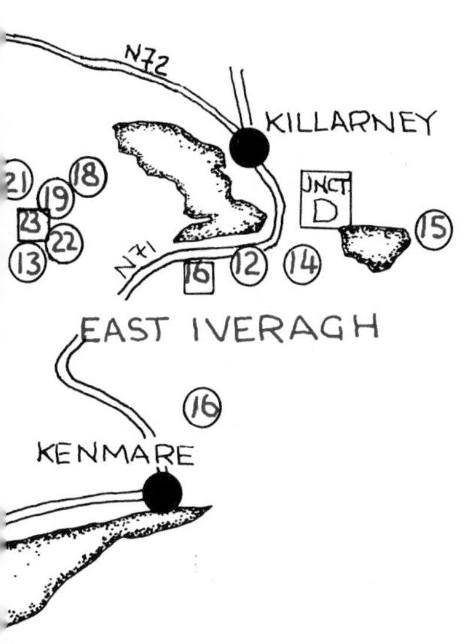

West Dingle p12
1 Great Blasket Island
2 *Brandon Point
3 *Mount Eagle
4 *Brandon from the Pater-noster Lakes
5 Brandon from the West
6 *Connor Pass to Gearhane
Other Approaches to Brandon

Central and East Dingle p25
7 Glennahoo to Anascaul
8 *Anascaul and Beenoskee
9 *Caherconree and Baurtegaum
10 *Connor Pass to Beenbo
11 *Circuit of Glanteenassig

East Iveragh p35
12 Old Kenmare Road
13 The Black Valley
14 Mangerton
15 *Bennaunmore
16 Peakeen and Knockanaguish
17 Knocklomena
18 *Purple Mountain Group
19 *The Eastern Reeks
20 The Beenkeragh Ridge
21 *Carrauntoohil from Hag's Glen
22 Reeks Ridge from Black Valley
23 *Broaghnabinnia and Stumpa Duloigh

North Iveragh p52
24 Coomasaharn Lakeshore
25 Seefin
26 *Glenbeigh Corries
27 Knocknadobar
28 Colly

South Iveragh p59
29 Coomavoher
30 Eagles Hill
31 *Coomcallee
32 Mullaghanattin from the South
33 Finnararagh from Cloon Lough
34 *Knocknagantee
35 Coomalougha Lough
36 Bolus Head
Symbols...................inside back cover.

* Routes with Major Variations

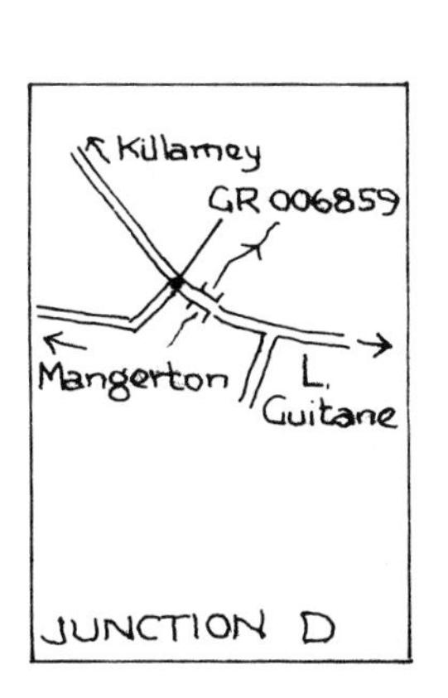

A QUICK LOOK AROUND

Kerry is situated in the far south-west of Ireland - if you are totally unfamiliar with the country you may recognise it on the map because of the long contorted fingers of land reaching westward into the Atlantic, which are at a glance anyway the distinguishing features of this area.

Of course it not just these long peninsulas which give it its special character. Far from it. The interplay of land and ocean is obvious enough, but it is the majestic mountains of the peninsulas and their rugged and unspoilt nature which make Kerry what it is.

The Dingle and Iveragh peninsulas, the area covered by this book, are two of the three main peninsulas in the county, the other being Beara to their south. Dingle is about 50km from east to west and culminates in Brandon, at 952m the highest mountain in Ireland outside Iveragh. Iveragh is much larger (about 60km along one axis and 25km along the other). As well as the Macgillycuddy's Reeks (a splendid name but hereinafter simply called the Reeks) which boast the highest mountains in Ireland virtually the entire peninsula offers excellent walking country.

At the start of each of the five sections of this book there is more about each of the fairly arbitrary areas (two in Dingle, three in Iveragh) into which the mountains are here divided.

HOW TO USE THIS BOOK

First of all, it is only fair to state that a map is needed in order to walk most of the routes in this book. More about suitable maps is given below and with each route description.

I have tried to cover all the best and most characteristic of the mountain areas in the region. Since the most characteristic are not necessarily the best, there had to be some compromises in choosing routes. I have taken a 'warts and all' approach; that is I do not describe everywhere and every route as being superlatively good. However it has to be said that Kerry has a bewildering array of superlatively good mountains to walk and a choice was very difficult. All routes detailed here have more than a few favourable characteristics but some are better (or should I say even better?) than others. My opinions are simply that - opinions- and yours might well be quite different.

The Sketch Maps: These accompany nearly all route descriptions and are sufficient for the easier walks only. Their aim is to emphasise what is *not* on the maps: cliffs, walls, fences etc. Features which are important for navigation or reassurance are shown in red. With one obvious exception these maps are on a scale of 1:50 000, that is the same as the most widely used Ordnance Survey (OS) maps. North is always to the top of the page. The symbols are explained on the inside back cover.

Before you set off on a walk it might be a good idea to pencil in the proposed route onto your map from the sketch map given here.

Grid References: These are the four- or six-digit numbers preceded by the letters 'GR', which appear in this book after some locations, particularly the starting points of routes. The figure uniquely identifies the location on most maps. The system is explained on all OS maps.

The following notes refer to each of the paragraphs which form the route description for each route.

'Getting There': To get to the starting point of many of these routes involves miles of travel on bad minor, and nearly as bad, major roads. Where it is not obvious an approximate time to get to the start of each route is given. There's more about this in 'Getting Around Kerry' below.

'Walking Time': This time is based on a variation of Naismith's Rule. It allows one hour for 4km on the flat plus one hour for each 500m of climbing. Thus a walk of 2km on the flat with a climb of 250m should take 1 hour. This is a fairly leisurely pace but it does not allow much time for eating, taking photographs or any other normal stops. Where justified this walking time is adjusted for difficult terrain (eg steep descents, rough vegetation) or easy terrain (eg good tracks).

'Difficulties': This is mostly self-explanatory, but note that wet ground can make routes much more difficult, especially routes which involve scrambling or clambering over rocks. Heavy rain might make streams which are normally fordable completely impassable.

'Map(s)' gives the best map(s) for the route. Where one is specified it is essential that it be taken. There is more about suitable maps below.

'Route': The place names used in this paragraph (and of course elsewhere) are those used on the OS Discovery Series maps or failing that the 1:25 000 maps, regardless of whether they are the commonly used versions. In the case of some names in Irish-speaking areas the more commonly used English version (as used on older maps) is used on first mention and thereafter the Irish version.

GETTING TO KERRY

The main roads are shown on any small-scale map and it is pointless to try to laboriously duplicate the information here.

The approximate distance and journey times by car to Killarney are:

from Dublin 190 miles / 300km (about 4½ hours),
from Rosslare Harbour 170 miles / 280km (about 4 hours),
from Galway 120 miles / 190km (about 2½ hours) and
from Cork 55 miles / 90km (about 1¼ hours).

Irish Bus/Bus Eireann run a number of express (ie limited stop) services into the region. The relevant timetable numbers are 13 and 14 from Dublin (about 6-7 hours); 40 from Rosslare Harbour (about 6½ hours); 42 and 50 from Cork (about 2½ hours); 44 from Cork via Skibbereen; 50 and 53 from Galway (5 hours).

There are rail stations in Killarney and Tralee with direct connections to Dublin and Cork.

The nearest international airport is at Shannon. There is a local airport at Farranfore between Tralee and Killarney, which offers regular flights from British cities.

GETTING AROUND KERRY

BY CAR

The principal road in the Dingle peninsula is the N86 which runs west from Tralee along the eastern end of the north side of the peninsula, then crosses diagonally over the high ground at the centre of the peninsula to terminate in

Dingle town. In this peninsula, Connor Hill Road offers high-level views over a great expanse of mountain territory.

In Iveragh the N70 runs right round the peninsula, hugging the coast for the most part and allowing comparatively high speeds in places. In other places, notably from Blackwater Bridge (GR 7968) to Waterville it facilitates those who have a leisurely approach to driving. The only other N-road is the N71 from Killarney to Kenmare which crosses high ground for much of its length and unsurprisingly, is narrow and winding.

There are few even moderately good stretches of road in the interior of the peninsula itself. The roads through the remote passes at Ballaghbeama (GR 7578) and Ballaghisheen (GR 6779) yield excellent views; passengers (only) will perforce have plenty of time to admire them. The status of the road through the Gap of Dunloe (south of GR 8888) is ambiguous: it is narrow and winding, is described as not suitable for cars on a notice at the northern end, where car occupants may also suffer hassle from local jarveys, nevertheless cars still use it. It is best to consider it off-limits except in an emergency.

It might also be worth noting that Ballaghisheen and Ballaghbeama, mentioned above, together with Glencar (GR 7284) are useful reference points often named on signposts, though strangely insignificant on most maps.

The signposting on these minor roads is poor. If you are new to Ireland you may not be aware of one hazard: some signs that are supported on a single post are twisted so as to send cars off in the wrong direction, a feature which makes all such signs suspect. In these unhappy circumstances it may be prudent to have a large-scale map and a navigator who can follow progress doggedly with a finger glued to the map. It's a nuisance to have to do this but better than the demoralisation engendered by getting lost even before you get out of the car!

Pages 2 and 3 include sketch maps of four sets of junctions (all in remote areas) that you will probably arrive at sooner or later in the course of your driving in Kerry - even if you didn't intend to. These sketch maps may be of use if you are uncertain which way to drive next.

BY BUS

Bus Eireann provides the only regular local bus service (a local bus will stop anywhere as long as it is safe to do so). Note that the timetable number ie the number under which the bus route appears in Bus Eireann timetable is not necessarily the same as the number (if any) which appears on the bus itself.

In the Dingle peninsula the relevant timetable numbers are 276, 277 which serve the western end of the peninsula with a variety of options on different days of the week; 275, 284 which serve Dingle town from Tralee and 281 which meanders all the way round the peninsula from Killarney.

In Iveragh the entire centre of the peninsula is without a regular bus service. There is a useful summer only, anti-clockwise service circumnavigating the entire peninsula (timetable 280). It runs on the N70 as far as Sneem, and then inland on the R568 and N71 to Killarney. The northern side of the N70 (between Waterville and Killorglin) is also served by the fairly frequent timetable 279 service and the southern side (between Sneem and Killarney via Kilgarvan) by the timetable 270 service. Note that these last two services tend to run eastward in the morning, an important point if you wish to walk A to B routes using the bus for one journey.

The only express buses which might be useful for getting to the start of routes are given in timetables 14 and 42, both of which stop at Beaufort Bridge (GR

8892) and possibly the 44, which travels between Killarney and Kenmare, unfortunately without stopping anywhere in between.

BY COACH OR TAXI

If you are a large party it may be more economical to use a coach or taxi rather than public transport. The firms providing such services are listed in the telephone directory.

BY BICYCLE

There are lots of places where bikes may be hired. Don't forget that, if you have only one car, you can use a bike to make A to B walks. As well as arranging that A and B are not too far apart, try to ensure that the bike journey will not be all uphill and that you are not cycling into the prevailing westerly winds.

HITCHHIKING

This is a time-honoured way of getting round all over rural Ireland. However, if you are dripping wet and carrying a bulky rucksack your chances will not be enhanced. Of course, this is just the time you will really want a lift! Women travelling alone after dark might be advised to avoid hitching.

ACCOMMODATION

There is lots of tourist accommodation ranging from camping to luxury hotel available in all areas of Kerry, with nearly all towns and villages offering a wide variety of board. Details are available from Bord Failte (see under 'Useful Contacts' below).

In the Dingle peninsula the most convenient location for hill walkers is probably Camp / Castlegregory (although Dingle town is the biggest on the peninsula it is situated comparatively far from the more rugged mountains to the north). Killarney is convenient for the eastern end of Iveragh, with Kenmare (also a good centre for Beara to the south), Sneem (a particularly attractive village), Waterville and Cahersiveen for other areas of that peninsula. And don't forget Glencar (GR 7284), a tiny village close to many excellent walking routes.

If you are relying on public transport the choice is pretty bleak: Dingle or Tralee for the Dingle peninsula and Killarney, Sneem, Waterville or Cahersiveen for Iveragh.

There is a youth hostel at the western end of the Dingle peninsula at Dunquin. In Iveragh there are hostels at Aghadoe just to the west of Killarney; at Loo Bridge to the east; in the remote Black Valley convenient to the Reeks; at Ballinskelligs and Valentia Island at the western end of the peninsula.

There are also numerous other hostels on both peninsulas (details from the address under 'Useful Contacts' below).

MAPS

The OS maps covering the entire Kerry region are excellent; in some places there is a even a good choice of acceptable maps.

The up-to-date 1:50 000 Discovery Series covers the region. Sheets 70 and 71, of which 70 is by far the more useful cover Dingle. Sheets 78 (of particular interest as it covers a large chunk of the best of the mountains), 79 (of marginal interest and at present only available in a preliminary series), 83 and 84 cover Iveragh. Much of the best walking country in Iveragh is also covered at 1:25

000 by the "Killarney National Park" and the "Macgillycuddy's Reeks" maps. It is doubtful if these 1:25 000 maps are worth buying except for parts of the Reeks, as the detail is little better than the 1:50 000 maps and they are unwieldy to use in bad weather. Finally Killarney National Park (west of Killarney) is covered by a small one-inch map produced by the National Parks authority, which wouldn't be worth mentioning were it not for the fact that it may be obtained for only a small charge.

Since most hill walkers will use the Discovery Series sheets it is worth while pointing out a few of their more important characteristics.

- Cliffs are not explicitly depicted, so you must use your judgement by noting the convergence of contour lines. Contour lines have been omitted altogether in the case of some sections of sea-cliff.
- Forests tend not to be as extensive as depicted.
- Many firebreaks are shown as forest tracks. In general, 'tracks' shown on the maps which ignore the lie of the land and are shown traversing hill and valley in straight lines are in fact firebreaks. Actual tracks tend to keep to gentle slopes and to wind in zig-zag fashion on steep ones.
- The thin black or grey lines shown in some upland areas are field boundaries of some kind, usually walls or earthbanks.
- Few paths or footbridges are shown. The long distance paths are badly depicted in places.
- The thickness of the lines used to indicate streams usually has little bearing on how wide they actually are.

Other maps may be dealt with more briefly. The old half-inch to the mile (1:126 720) series is no longer published, though you may be able to buy copies of the relevant sheets (20, 21, 24). They are of use in getting to the start of routes, though of little use on the route itself except on the easier routes in good visibility. There is also a 1:250 000 map (Holiday Map, sheet 4), which is useful for overall planning.

LONG DISTANCE PATHS

There are waymarked long distance paths traversing both peninsulas. The Dingle Way begins in Tralee and forms a loop around the peninsula. About 155km long, its highest point is a considerable 660m at the western end of the peninsula. The Kerry Way is about 215km long and is thus the longest of all the Republic's long distance paths. Starting in Killarney, it loops around Iveragh and in addition has two sub-loops. Strip maps for both long distance paths have been published by Cork/Kerry Tourism.

A FEW ROUTE SELECTIONS

Here is a selection of routes for particular purposes.

If you have a limited number of days and want a varied selection try these routes:

In Dingle routes 3, 4, 9 (maybe the short variation) and 11.

In East Iveragh routes 15, 17, 20, 21.

In North and South Iveragh routes 26, 28, 32, 34, 35.

If you want short routes try 1, 2, 4 (variation), 9 (variation), 12, 13, 15 (variations), 16, 24, 25, 27, 29, 35, 36.

If you want routes which might be walked from the long distance paths:
From the Dingle Way try routes 2, 9 (variation).
From the Kerry Way try routes 12, 16, 25, 30, 34.

SAFETY

Walkers unused to Irish (and British) conditions will be excused if they are asked to read carefully a section on safety, given that the highest mountain in the entire region (and the country) is a puny 1039m.

Do not be misled by such seemingly insignificant heights! Irish mountains in general (and this region is no exception) are wild, remote and worthy of respect. It is noteworthy that a high proportion of the fatal accidents in recent years has been suffered by visitors who did not realise the conditions they were to face.

But let's not be too timid. If you take reasonable precautions and do not try walking in conditions for which you are unprepared, you will enjoy your time in the mountains and return to base safely and with a sense of having achieved something worthwhile.

So, what are reasonable precautions?

- You will get some idea of what to expect on each route from the section on 'Difficulties'. Of course, conditions vary greatly depending on the weather but you can assume that unless the route is entirely or almost entirely on road, track or path you should wear walking boots.
- The section on 'Difficulties' will also give you an idea of how hard it will be to find your way round the route, but remember that the easiest route to follow in bad visibility may be harder than the hardest in good. Cloud and fog make all the difference to navigation. As well as the obvious lack of visibility they are disorienting and distorting, so that what is in reality a minor hill near at hand will appear through cloud like a major mountain much further away.
- It is definitely prudent not to walk alone and better to have at least four persons. This allows one to stay with the victim if there is an accident and two to try to get help. If the worst comes to the worst, you can summon the mountain rescue by phoning 999.
- Leave word at base of where you intend to go and what time you intend to be back.
- Don't forget to get a weather forecast before you go. You can get one for the area by phoning 1550 123 850.

WHAT TO CARRY WITH YOU

If you were to carry all the equipment that some experts advise you to carry, you would be so weighed down that you wouldn't be able to walk.

The most important item to get right are boots, as mentioned in the section 'Safety' above. Apart from that there are only a few thing that you really must carry. These include food and a flask with a hot liquid, a whistle and a map and compass. Map and compass are no good unless you know how to use them! Unless the day looks uncommonly settled and likely to remain so, you should take a waterproof. Lastly, you need a rucksack to put everything else in. Anything else is optional or depends mainly on the weather and the route.

RIGHTS OF WAY AND GOOD CONDUCT

Nearly all the land over which you walk in this region, the major exceptions being Killarney National Park and the waymarked paths, belongs to someone and you are his or her uninvited guest. Landowners are generally trusting folk and will not object to your walking across their land. Do not abuse the privilege - and that is what it is. Remember this and behave accordingly. Specifically:

- Do not bring dogs into sheep rearing country, that is nearly everywhere in the mountains.
- Do not stand on fence wire. It may look the same afterwards but will have been irretrievably damaged. If you have to cross stone walls, make sure you do not dislodge any stones.
- Leave gates, open or closed, just as you found them. If you have to climb gates, do so at the hinged end.
- Do not litter the mountains - or anywhere else for that matter. You would be doing a singular service to other hill walkers if you would remove some litter that you find in remote areas such as mountain summits.
- Exchange a few words with farmers you encounter. It's amazing what you may learn about local history or snippets of local lore.

THEY'RE YOUR MOUNTAINS - GET INVOLVED!

I wish I could say that the beauty of Ireland's mountains was reflected in the care and attention that we, the Irish people, pay to our environment. Alas, it isn't. There is no need to elaborate, except to state that because I have usually not mentioned specific instances of littering and dumping in these pages does not mean that I have not noticed them or have not been saddened by them. Kerry, by the way, seems to be no worse than most areas in Ireland and a lot better than some.

Would that there were a simple solution to this problem, which is caused both by an ingrained couldn't-care-less attitude on the part of too many people and an unwillingness on the part of the responsible authorities to enforce laws. All I can suggest here is that you get involved in any organisation which tries to look after the environment and that if you are in a walking club that you ensure that there is an active conservation group and get involved in it.

Carrauntoohil from the Bone (Route 21)

USEFUL CONTACTS

Irish Youth Hostel Association / An Oige, 61 Mountjoy Street, Dublin 7. ☎ 01-830 4555.
Irish Bus / Bus Eireann, Casement Stn, Tralee. ☎ 066-23566.
Irish Rail / Iarnrod Eireann. For general information on all rail services ☎ 01-836 6222. For information on services into Tralee and Killarney ☎ 01-855 4466.
Irish Tourist Board / Bord Failte. There are all-year offices at:
Denny Street, Tralee (☎ 066-21288)
Town Hall, Killarney (☎ 064-31633)
There are seasonal offices in Dingle (phone 066-51188), Cahersiveen (☎ 066-72589), Glencar (☎ 066-60101) and Kenmare (☎ 064-41233).
Independent Holiday Hostels, 58 Lr. Gardiner Street, Dublin 1. ☎ 01-836 4700.
Ordnance Survey Office, Phoenix Park, Dublin 8. ☎ 01-820 6100.
Mountaineering Council of Ireland, House of Sport, Longmile Road, Dublin 12. ☎ 01-450 9845.
Mountain Rescue ☎ 999.

WEST DINGLE

West Dingle is dominated by the Brandon massif of which Brandon Mountain (don't confuse it with Brandon Peak) at 952m is the highest (routes 2, 4-6). A long series of corries topped by mighty cliffs dominates its eastern side, while on the west and north it drops more gently to cliffs facing the ocean. Brandon is one of the highest mountains in Ireland, and more to the point, the whole massif of which this is the focus offers splendid, varied walking. Other walking in this area (routes 1, 3) is much more gentle and gives excellent views of the coast and its off-shore islands.

ROUTE 1: GREAT BLASKET ISLAND

The sea-cliffs bounding Great Blasket, whose whale-like profile reaches south-west oceanwards, dominate a scattering of lesser islands around. With springy turf underfoot and excellent views over island and ocean, this is an easy, most enjoyable walk. But Great Blasket is much more than a walk: it is a journey into a simple, self-sufficient and hard way of life and a culture, now extinct but one of the last to survive in the western world (1).

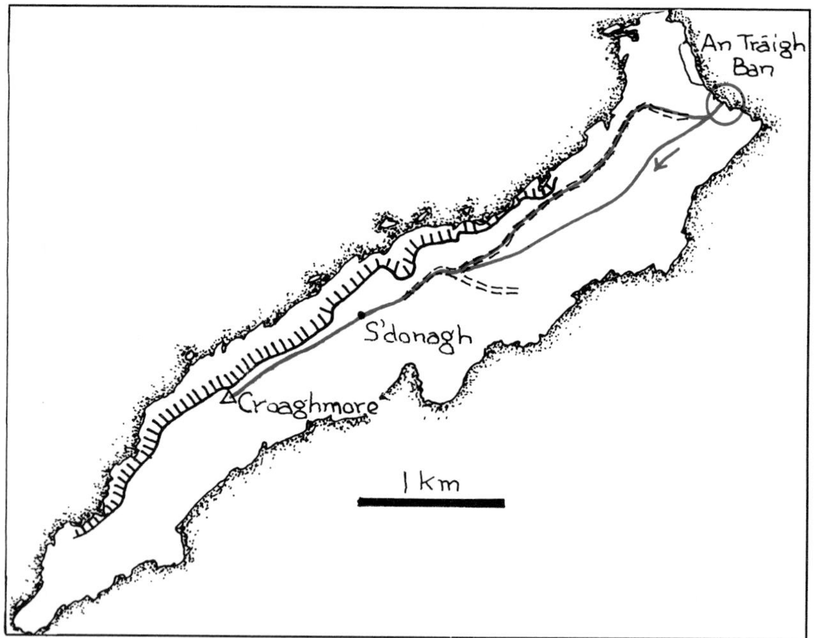

Getting There: A ferry sails from Dunquin Pier (GR 315997), about 10 miles (16km) west of Dingle. To get there turn at the sign off the R559 (Slea Head Drive) and park in the carpark on the left only a few hundred metres from the junction. From the carpark walk down steep steps to the ferry. At present (1996) there are two sailings each way per day and the cost is £10. For further information phone Dingle tourist office (see 'Useful Contacts' in Introduction).
Buses: Timetables 276, 281 to Dunquin.
Walking Time: 2.75 hours (distance 8km, climb 500m).
Difficulties: None.
Map: None necessary but take sheet 70 if you have it.

Route: This is really a pottering area and this is only one suggestion. The main thing is to be in time for the return boat!

From the landing point (at GR 283976) just to the east of An Tráigh Bhán walk south-west between the houses of the village to reach the high spine of the island. From here it is simply a matter of continuing south-west along the spine until you reach a definite saddle with a junction of tracks traversing it. Continue along the high ground with great grassy cliffs now on the right.

If you have the time it is worthwhile walking to the highest point on the island, Croaghmore (292m, 1.75 hours), from where a marvellous panorama of ocean and off-shore island awaits: Inishnabro ahead with Inishvickillane to its left, Tearaght to the west (it's the most westerly point in Ireland), Inishtooskeret to the north and far off to the south the two triangles of the Skelligs. And that's only the islands! Add to it the mountain ranges of Dingle and Iveragh and you have a scene which should live in your memory.

Note

(1) You should visit the interpretative centre in Dunquin before you go to the island. It gives much fascinating information about the way of life on the Blaskets while they were still permanently inhabited.

ROUTE 2: BRANDON POINT

North of the Brandon massif a great line of cliffs faces ocean-ward, indented only at the great amphitheatre of Sauce Creek, where steep ground plunges 350m to a barely accessible cove. The walk reaches this memorable point and also traverses two remote valleys facing directly to the ocean. After all this, the return along the Dingle Way is tame indeed!

Getting There: Drive to Cloghane (GR 5011), continue northwards along the coast road for about 4 miles (7km) to reach a carpark at the end of the road (GR 527173). The total distance from Tralee is about 26 miles (42km), but seems longer.

Walking Time: 4.5 hours (distance 13km, climb about 650m), though many variations are possible (see below). For the sake of the views make sure that you reach Sauce Creek.

Difficulties: Navigation easy. Some of the underfoot conditions are fairly rough, particularly at the height of summer when bracken is rampant.

Map: Sheet 70 though it is hardly needed in good weather.

Route: Cross the gate at the carpark, follow the track beyond for a minute or so and then leave it to follow the line of the cliffs westward (you will meet the track again a little later on).

From here until the first valley encountered the route is of necessity a bit vague as there is no obvious route. It's probably best not to climb too high above the cliffs since I recommend that you cross the first valley near its seaward (and therefore lower) end. The only recognisable landmark along this first stretch of coast is Deelick Point, where a tiny peninsula of bare red rock looks like a submarine beached off the cliffs. The first valley, which seems a thousand miles from anywhere, is a lovely place for a break. A stream hastening over boulders and sandstone slabs before its plunge seaward is its focus; to its east and west it is hemmed in by steep ground, with the pounding ocean stretching away to the north.

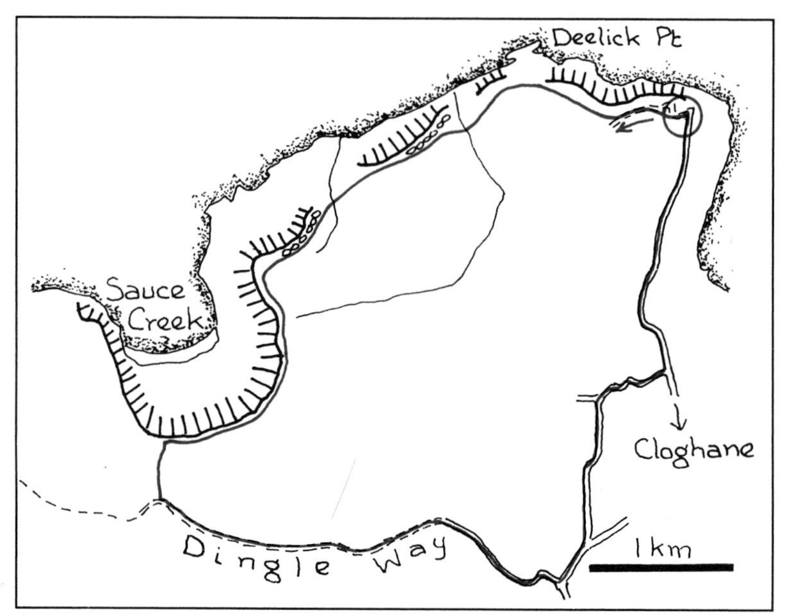

When you have summoned up sufficient energy to drag yourself away, climb steeply following a wall or boundary stones - there is little question now of a lower alternative since steep, rocky ground faces the ocean from here on as far as the second valley a few hundred metres away.

I expect you imagine this valley to be as attractive as the first. Well, it isn't! I find it hard to figure out why exactly: maybe it is not as defined a valley, the underfoot conditions are not as pleasant, certainly the stream is less attractive. With therefore less reason to linger you can more easily face the next task, the climb south-westward to the edge of Sauce Creek.

This is unmistakable and dramatic, a huge bowl of cliffs and steep ground nearly a kilometre across and 350m deep and with a tiny beach and flat area (on which surprisingly, there are remains of walls) sandwiched between cliffs and ocean. Though I haven't done so it looks as if it is easy enough to make one's way to the beach from at least one place along the cliff edge.

Walk south and west along the sides of the Creek, after which, with about 2 hours walking still to do, you may like to head for home (but see the variations below). To do so head south from the south-west corner of the Creek (the exact point is immaterial) to reach a track - it's also the Dingle Way. The Way is incorrectly depicted on sheet 70, being drawn further north than it actually is.

Once on the Way the rest is easy: a track yields to narrow roads and a convoluted route around Brandon village. Convoluted, that is for those walking the Way; if your car is back at the carpark it isn't. Simply follow the Way to the coast road, turn left and walk the 2km to the start.

Variations: If you have two cars it might be better to park one carefully in Brandon village (GR 5214) in order to minimise the road walk at the end.

If you have time you could explore the cliffs and tiny valleys west of Sauce Creek, climb Masatiompan and then descend to the Dingle Way at its highest point (GR 4614). The main route above can be used as a more interesting alternative to the Dingle Way.

The Hags Glen (Route 21)

ROUTE 3: MOUNT EAGLE

An easy ascent to Mount Eagle (516m) with lovely seaward views to the Blaskets and the Skelligs and with a variety of surfaces underfoot: road, track and some pathless, wet terrain.

Getting There: Park in the carpark that is tucked below the high ground at the base of Dunmore Head (GR 312982) and just off the R559 (Slea Head road). From here Dingle is about 11 miles (18km) to the east. If you have a non-walking driver you can omit the road walk on the R559 (though it is quite scenic - so much so that most of it is also the route of the Dingle Way). **Buses:** Timetables 276, 281. Bus variations are given below.

Walking Time: 3.75 hours (distance 11km, climb 520m).

Difficulties: None, except for some boggy terrain north of Mount Eagle.

Map: Sheet 70.

Route: Walk north from the carpark, following the R559. Pass the school on the left and a few hundred metres further on fork right uphill off the R559. There is a stiff climb before you take the first turn right onto a track.

From here the scenery begins to open out in all directions revealing a wide range of coastal, island and mountain scenery, as well as the long, laboriously-made fields climbing up the steep slopes of Mount Eagle. The track zig-zags steeply uphill, and eventually reaches level ground at a tee on boggy ground north of the summit. Turn right here to head towards it.

Rather than follow the track all the way to within a few hundred metres of the summit, it is worthwhile diverting left from it to walk along the edge of the corrie containing Mount Eagle Lough. Where the cliffs begin to swing to the

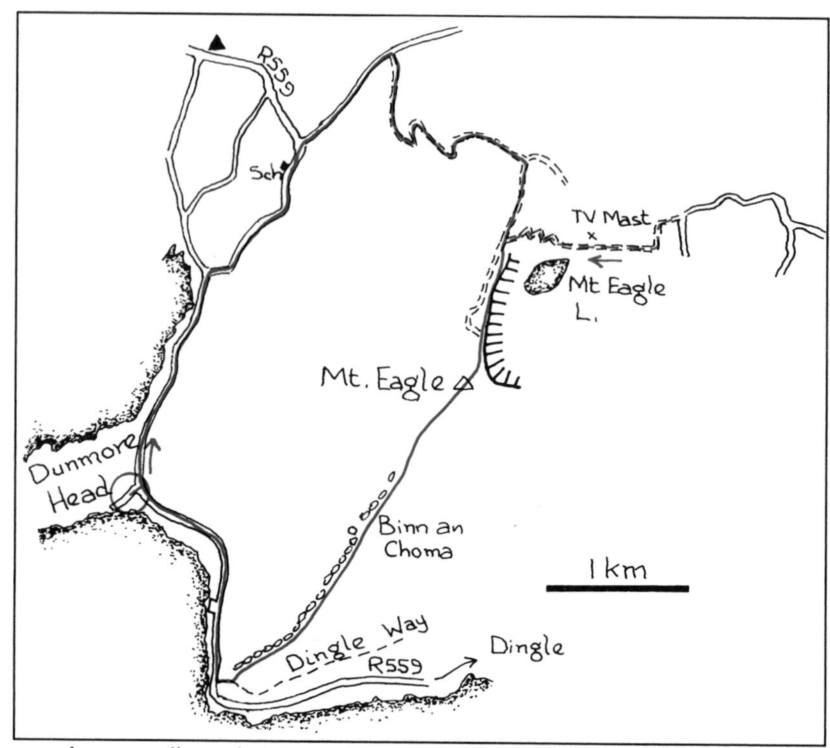

south-east, walk south-west to the summit of Mount Eagle (516m), which is crowned by a trig pillar but otherwise undistinguished. Head about south-west on the descent aiming for the crest of the long spur reaching to Binn an Choma and beyond. Along here the views of the Blaskets, the unmistakable triangles of the Skelligs off to the south and a great expanse of mountain on the Dingle and Iveragh peninsulas make for a memorable panorama. As you descend you should pick up a line of boundary stones, graduating to an intermittent wall which heads all the way down. Don't worry if you cannot find Binn an Choma, which is named on the map but not apparent on the ground.

Your descent will be abruptly terminated directly above the Slea Head road by decidedly steeper ground and a fence. This is the route of the Dingle Way (it may not be immediately obvious), onto which you should turn right to reach the road. The carpark is about 1km away to the right.

Alternative routes by bus. If you are staying in Dingle take the timetable 276 service to Ventry Church. Walk up to the village of Kildurrihy, take the track from there via the TV mast to the summit plateau. Walk the above route to the Dingle Way, then follow the Way back to Ventry or Dingle.

This alternative route may also be easily adapted to reach the youth hostel in Dunquin.

Slieveanea (670m) (Route 10)

ROUTE 4: BRANDON FROM THE PATER-NOSTER LAKES

A classic! From the initial demanding ascent up rocky slopes, each ending at a mountain lochan nestling between progressively closer and mightier cliffs, to the summit of Brandon Mountain itself (952m) and the subsequent walk along the jagged edge of the Brandon massif, each step of the way reveals new delights. Only the final, tiring descent disappoints a little - but only in comparison with what has gone before. A tough but highly memorable walk.

Getting There: The start is about 25 miles (40km) from Tralee and about 12 miles (19km) from Dingle. From Tralee follow the N86 initially, continue straight ahead on the R560 where the N86 swings left, and then follow signs for Cloghane (Clochán). Just before the village watch out carefully! Cross a bridge, noting the Garda (police) station on the right just beyond it, cross another bridge and take the next left. Drive from here for 2.0 miles (3.2km) to cross two adjacent bridges (GR 490084). Park anywhere on the side of the road after these bridges.

From Dingle take the road over Connor Pass, then follow signs towards Cloghane, thus eventually arriving at the first of the bridges before the village.

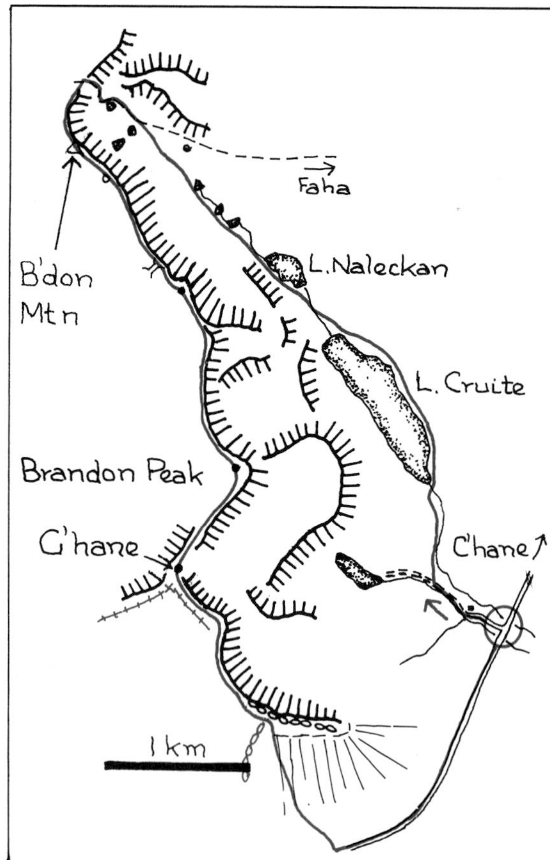

Walking Time: 7 hours (distance 14km, climb 1140m), thus allowing nearly an hour extra for rough terrain on the ascent and a half-hour for a steep descent at the end.

Difficulties: Easy navigation and good underfoot conditions. However, take care on the last steep descent.

Map: Sheet 70.

Route: Take the track whose junction with the road is between the two bridges, walk to the farmhouse and ask permission of the friendly people there to continue. Closing gates carefully behind you, continue up the track for a few hundred metres, noting ahead the fine corrie from which a waterfall gushes. That's not the way you're going!

Instead, watch out for a stream descending from

your right and at any convenient point head towards it and follow it upstream, crossing fences carefully. It doesn't matter which bank you walk but you are aiming to walk alongside the north-east side of the lakes ahead. However even if you elect to walk the western bank you can cross the causeway at Loch Cruite (Lough Cruittia), the first of the lakes in the pater-noster string.

This lake is the largest of all on the route. It's a marvellous location: a long, jagged line of cliffs on its south-west side and the great corrie climbing skyward to the north-west. And remember, the lakes along this corrie are just as scenic as this one.

There's a steep but short climb to the next lake, Lough Nalacken, and an equally short but steeper climb over sloping slabs to the next (only one lake from here is named on the maps). This climb is best undertaken with the waterfall, one of several on this stretch, on your right. After which little need be said, as you will be channelled along the boulder-strewn bottom of the narrowing corrie. As for the scenery and the ambience .... it's nothing short of stupendous!

Near the end of the corrie you will notice the path from Faha marching gently down the grassy slope on the right. You will eventually join it in a comparatively level area where there are several lakes at various levels (around here are the last spots at which you can stock up with water). From here on follow the path which climbs the corrie wall and which, in spite of its steepness, should not cause vertigo.

This path ends abruptly at the top of the cliffs. Turn left here to walk a few hundred metres (distance) and 70m or so (climb) to the trig pillar, just one of the items on the summit of Brandon Mountain (952m, 4 hours). From the summit, the highest point in Ireland outside the Reeks, you can see the great line of cliffs reaching to north and south, the mountains of the rest of the peninsula to the east and in stark contrast, a comparatively gentle moorland, ending at a line of sea-cliffs to north-west and west, beyond which are a scattering of islands of which Great Blasket is the largest and the Skelligs the most distinctive. At least, I hope you see all this, because the summit is frequently shrouded in cloud: as they say in these parts, 'it wears its cap'. If visibility is good, you could hardly hope for a more majestic scene, one that you will enjoy from varying angles all the way along the cliff edge.

The next goal is Brandon Peak. Walk south-east from the summit with the cliffs on the left. Navigationally this is easy: there are two comparatively minor tops on the generally downward trend. You don't have to climb them - but don't mistake them for Brandon Peak (840m) itself, which is preceded by a sustained climb of 90m (the other two climbs are not more than 30m each).

From Brandon Peak walk south to Gearhane (803m). While the cliffs ease on this stretch there is still a narrow, but grassy, not quite knife-edge ridge just before the summit which might be a useful indication of your position in bad visibility. Just south of Gearhane is a strange sight for this height: a gate with accompanying fences. Keep to the left of these and you will be guided down the south-east spur of Gearhane over easy ground.

After about 1km from the summit of Gearhane, and still close to a cliff on the left, note the stone wall heading directly away from it. Continue downhill along the cliff for another few minutes, but then gradually veer away from it. The reason for this is that if you continue along the cliff you will end up in a dreadful area of dense vegetation and hidden rocks - just what you don't need at this late stage of the walk. The route suggested here is not all that easy, with rocks and steep ground to negotiate, but it is a lot better than the alternative.

At length you will reach the road, a cul-de-sac deep in the lonely valley of the Cloghane River. Turn left here and walk about 1.5km to the start.

Much Shorter Variation. Walk at least as far as the first lake, Loch Cráite, taking in Loch an Mhónáin on the way. You will see the waterfall issuing from this lake shortly after you have passed the farmhouse.

ROUTE 5: BRANDON FROM THE WEST

A gradual and unrelenting climb to the cliff edge south of Brandon Mountain is followed by an exhilarating walk of about 3km along that cliff. The return is along the Dingle Way and lowland tracks and roads.

Getting There: The start is at the village of An Baile Breac (Ballybrack) (GR 4209), about 6 miles (10km) north of Dingle and easily reached from there. There are signs for Brandon Mountain close to the village.

Walking Time: 5.25 hours (distance 15km, climb about 1000m).

Difficulties: Underfoot conditions are generally good. Take care to take the correct turnings on the minor roads and tracks near the end of the route.

Map: Sheet 70.

Route: From the dilapidated sign at the eastern (far) end of the village warning of the great dangers that are about to threaten you, take the track beyond and walk .... and walk ... and walk. Track yields to path, marker stones or cairns. If you happen to lose these indications keep walking north-east and you will doubtless pick them up again.

Rather than walk directly to the summit of Brandon Mountain I suggest you swing east after climbing for about 1.75 hours (there is a standing stone about here) with the aim of reaching a low point on the cliff edge about 1km away (for the academically minded the col is at GR 467107). Once at the cliff turn left and head for Brandon Mountain (3 hours), taking in one minor top on the way. (There is more about this section of the walk under route 4.)

From the summit continue north along another lovely section of cliff, climbing the short distance to pt 891m and then passing the cliffs overlooking An Loch Dubh. After this follow the high ground to the curious steep-sided, rocky knob of Piaras Mór (Pierasmore) and, with massive Masatiompan now looming ahead, walk north to an Ogham Stone and the Dingle Way - at 660m the highest point of the Way.

Turn left here and walk all the way (and Way) to tarmac. Continue on the Way for about another kilometre but where the Way takes a right angle bend to the right continue straight ahead, still on a minor road.

Continue south on this road until it in turn swings abruptly right. Here a decision. If you fear muddy boots take the road back to An Baile Breac; the route is obvious from the map. If you have no such fears keep straight ahead on a track. It is here that you are most likely to make navigational errors since there are several sub-tracks and would-be tracks heading off vaguely. Just keep doggedly south until you reach An Baile Breac - you're bound to get there eventually!

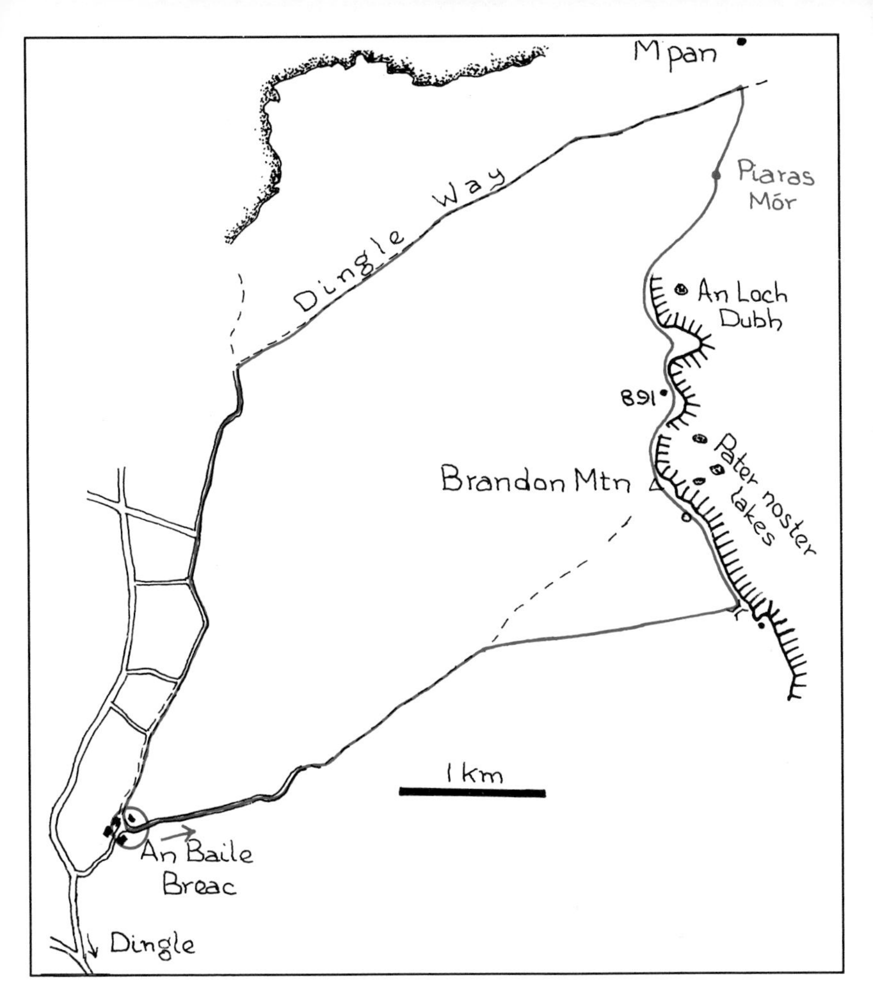

ROUTE 6: CONNOR PASS TO GEARHANE

A route which has a high starting point for a climb to Brandon Mountain itself (see the variation), though the main route is not an altogether convincing circuit. The initial walk leads along the rims of rocky corries to lofty Gearhane (803m), a southern outlier of the Brandon massif. A steep, tough descent is followed by a slightly less tough ascent on track back to the start.

Getting There: Park at Connor Pass carpark (GR 4905). It's about 4 miles (6km) north-east of Dingle and 22 miles (35km) west of Tralee. If more convenient you can park near the end of the minor road running south from Cloghane at about GR 4807, an approach detailed under route 4.

Walking Time: 5.25 hours (distance 13km, climb 1000m), allowing about 0.25 hours extra for one steep descent. The route can easily be shortened.

Difficulties: Navigationally easy and good underfoot, so this is not a difficult route. There is however a psychological problem: a steep ascent at the end, a time when you would normally expect a nice, easy finish. The alternative starting point avoids this problem.

Map: Sheet 70.
Route: From the carpark head west. All the way to the major col beyond Ballysitteragh the ground underfoot is firm, there is no great climb or drop, navigation is easy (keep the cliffs on the right and follow the fence) and the views down into the three corries to the north and beyond to the Brandon massif are magnificent. So, stride out. The only comments I would make are that you will have to swing left on Beennabrack, an indistinct top, to keep to the cliff edge (the fence will guide you) and that you can climb Ballysitteragh (623m) if you are intent on climbing every hill within reach, but it is a non-event, a boggy plateau and hardly worth the diversion from the cliff edge.

After Ballysitteragh the route veers gradually from north-west to north, the cliff eases and there is a distinct drop to a col, where a waymarked route down to the right provides a short cut. For the main route continue northwards to pt 623m overlooking Loch na mBan, where it may be some interest to know that you are back at exactly the same height as Ballysitteragh.

A broad, gently sloping plain now presents itself, culminating in Gearhane to the north-east (there is also an agricultural road here - it is shown on the sketch

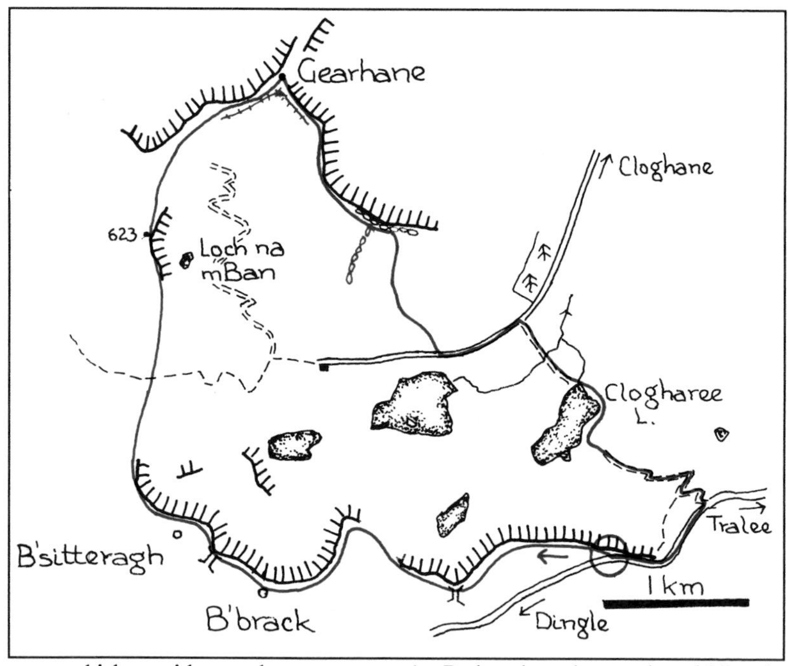

map - which provides another escape route). Rather than slog up the middle of the plain, contour from pt 623m to cliffs and follow their edge up to an improbably located gate set in a fence corner. Just beyond is the summit of Gearhane (803m, 3 hours) itself. If you have time and the day is good it will be hard to resist the temptation to push on to Brandon Mountain, a lovely walk (see below).

From the summit return to the gate and keeping it and the associated fences on the right walk south-east to a nearby section of cliff - yes, yet another - this one on the left. Cross a wall which heads to the right downhill and keep cliffs close on the left for another few minutes. Then begin to veer from the cliff edge, so heading south with a touch of east. As explained under route 4, this is to avoid difficult terrain on the direct descent, but it is steep and rocky even so.

When you eventually reach the road, the one which runs deep into the heart of the valley holding the Cloghane River, turn left and walk to within 100m or so of a plantation of sorry-looking stunted conifers. Here take a track on the right to cross the Cloghane River and a tributary of it, which issue from two lakes on the valley floor. The second of these lakes is Clogharee Lough and it is from here that you can ascend to Connor Hill Road now looming alarmingly high above you.

There is a track running from near this lake, but not from its shore. In good weather it will be fairly obvious. However don't head directly towards the zig-zag path which you can probably see just below Connor Pass (it branches high up from the track you are looking for). This path certainly gets to within a few tens of metres of the pass. Only trouble is, these tens of metres are vertical (1). The track you want ends well to the left of this. In good weather it is obvious: in bad, walk along the lake shore until you are within 100m or so of the lake's inlet stream, which tumbles down the steep slope from near Connor Pass. Walk roughly east from here and you will pick it up easily.

Walk up this track, passing close to Lough Beirne near the road. Continue on to the road, turn right and walk less than a kilometre to the carpark.

Variation to Brandon Mountain. A simple and memorable there-and-back from Gearhane which might take 1.5 hours there and 1.25 hours back, depending on whether you climb two tops on the way as well as Brandon Peak.

Note

(1) This road seems to have been the bright idea of a local landlord in the eighteenth century. The road made a beeline for the Connor Pass but then came unstuck, with impossible gradients, close to the pass itself.

OTHER APPROACHES TO BRANDON

Here are outlines of three other routes to and from Brandon Mountain.

Brandon Mountain from Connor Pass (GR 4905) (see also route 6): Walk over Ballysitteragh, Gearhane and Brandon Peak. Walking time to Brandon is 4 hours (distance 9km, climb 980m) and 3 hours (climb 440m) on the return, though these climbs may be reduced a little by omitting minor tops.

Brandon Mountain from Brandon Point (GR 5217): Take route 2 to Sauce Creek, walk the Dingle Way to its highest point (GR 4614) then take part of route 5 in reverse to Brandon. Walking time to Brandon is 5 hours (distance 11km, climb 1200m) and 3.5 hours (climb 340m) on the return. This route to Brandon is probably too long for most mortals, but you can take the Dingle Way from near Brandon village (it's worthwhile detouring to Sauce Creek) and so considerably reduce this time.

Brandon Mountain from Faha (GR 4911): Faha is well signposted from

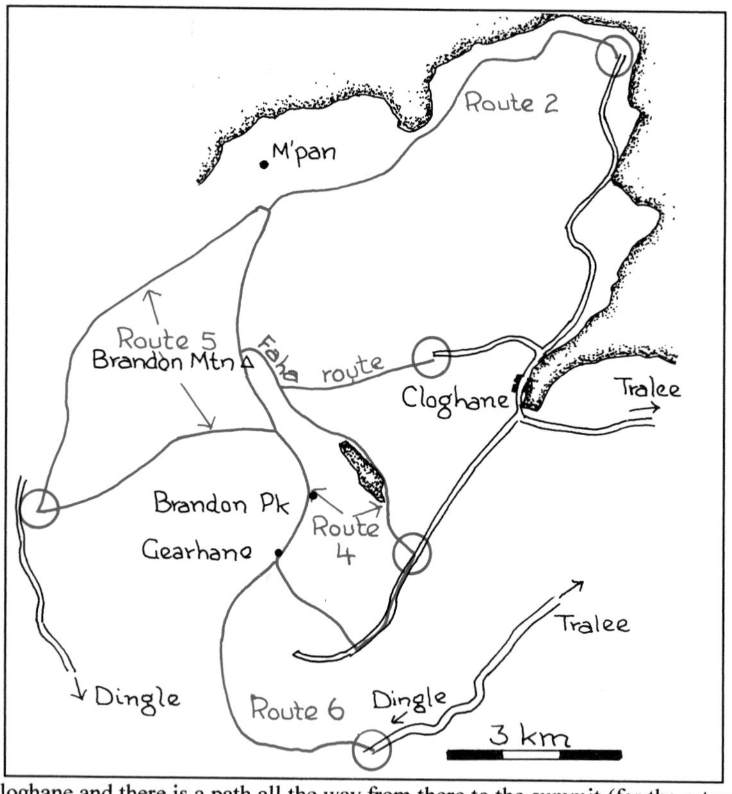

Cloghane and there is a path all the way from there to the summit (for the return, note that there is a sign just north of Brandon Mountain indicating the top of the path down to the pater-noster corrie). This is not a particularly interesting route for the first 2km or so but improves dramatically once the pater-noster corrie comes into view. Walking time to Brandon is 2.5 hours (distance 4km, climb 820m) and 1.25 hours for the return.

CENTRAL AND EAST DINGLE

Central and East Dingle, the area to the east of Connor Pass, consists of two ranges, Stradbally (826m) and Slieve Mish (851m). The Stradbally range (routes 7, 8, 10, 11) yields some excellent walks around a line of small corries and associated lakes, most of which face north over Tralee Bay. The best part of the Slieve Mish range (route 9) is that around Caherconree, where there are impressive river gorges and corries. Otherwise it is rather dull and gently sloping, especially on its southern side.

ROUTE 7: GLENNAHOO TO ANASCAUL

An easy walk across the peninsula, but not climbing the summits of any mountains. Road or track all the way reaching a modestly high point (360m). A long, narrow, grassy valley to start, then moorland, ending along the scenic shores of Lough Anascaul and on a minor road into Anascaul.

Getting There: Coming from the Tralee direction the start is at a side road off Connor Hill Road 1.2 miles (1.9km) south-west of the junction to Cloghane (GR 544102). Here the road takes a U-turn to the right; the side road is just before it. Cars are not allowed to park here so you will have to seek a place on the verge a little further on.

The finish is in Anascaul village (GR 5901), where there are pubs and a bus service (timetables 275, 281).

Walking Time: 3.5 hours (distance 12km, climb 320m).

Difficulties: None.

Map: Sheet 70.

Route: Take the side road south into Glennahoo. It soon becomes a track which runs the length of the valley, and then climbs steeply into a narrow sub-valley before reaching its highest point (here it is no more than a path) with Beenoskee to the north-east.

Walk downhill generally south-east on what is once again a track. It zig-zags down into the valley, which is bound east and west by the cliffs that hold Lough Anascaul. Take the road starting at the lakeside all the way into Anascaul.

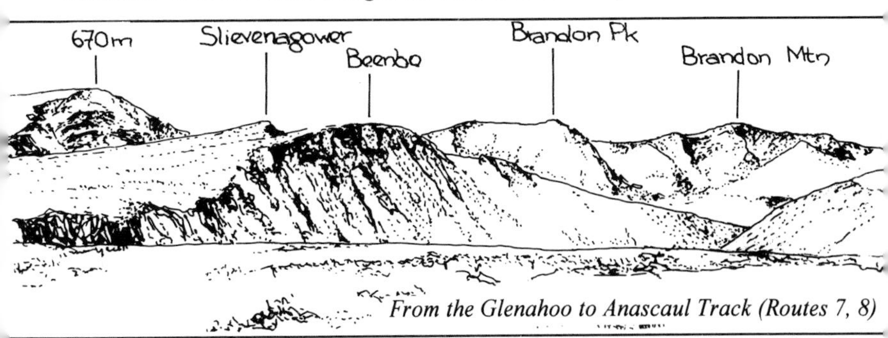

From the Glenahoo to Anascaul Track (Routes 7, 8)

ROUTE 8: ANASCAUL AND BEENOSKEE

Scenic Lough Anascaul is set in a bowl hemmed in on two sides by huge wedges of stern cliffs. The route climbs steeply out of this bowl to traverse the top of cliffs overlooking the wooded valley of Glanteenassig, before tackling the twin peaks of Stradbally and Beenoskee. The return is initially over dull terrain though with continuing magnificent longer views. Finally a downhill track through pleasant terrain overlooking Lough Anascaul leads back to the start.

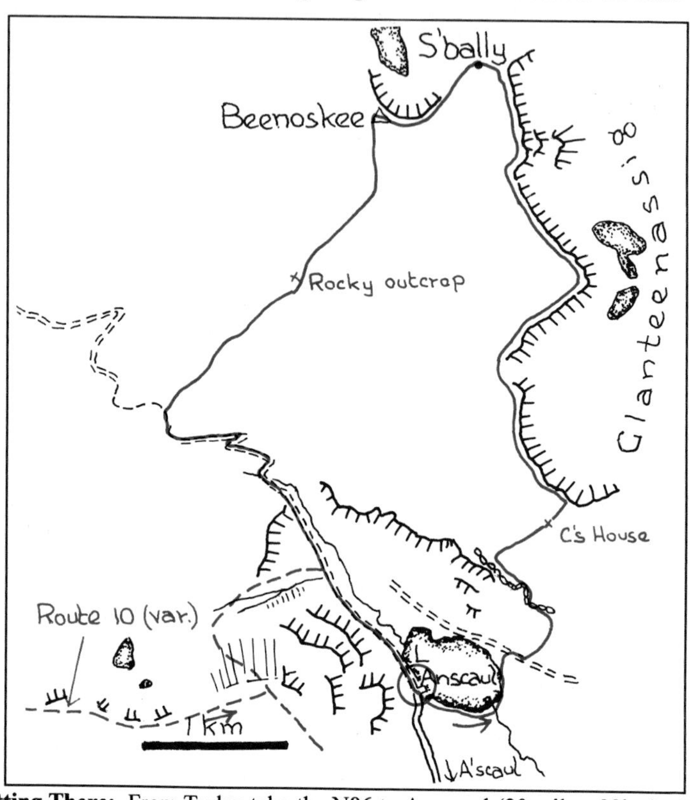

Getting There: From Tralee take the N86 to Anascaul (20 miles, 32km). From Dingle take the N86 to Anascaul (11 miles, 18km). In either case take the road signposted to Lough Anascaul. This means that from the Tralee direction cross the bridge at the far end of the village and turn first right. Drive to the lakeside carpark less than 3 miles (4km) further on (GR 583052). **Buses:** Timetables 275 and 281 buses serve Anascaul.

Walking Time: 5.25 hours (distance 13km, climb 1000m) though the climb in particular may be greatly reduced.

Difficulties: With the first kilometre or so behind you, you will have little to worry about. After rain it may be a problem to cross the none too useful stepping stones across the outlet stream from Lough Anascaul, which is wide but usually shallow (the inlet stream won't be much better). Then comes a steep climb through an area which may have bracken in high summer and is topped by a difficult fence. After all that nothing will seem difficult!

If you don't fancy this start you can walk up the track for about 2km (thus duplicating the end of the route) and tackle the cliffs on the north-east of Lough Anascaul from here.

Map: Sheet 70. If you have a presentiment that you are going to get lost to the east of the route take sheet 71 as well.

Route: Walk back from the carpark and crossing one fence with care, make your way along the shores of the lake to cross the outlet stream by the user-hostile stepping stones. Then walk up to a track running along the northern shore of the lake and contemplate for a moment the way ahead.

The goal is obvious enough: to climb steeply through the fields opposite. Trouble is, if you walk up through the abandoned field on the left you will find it topped by a barbed wire fence which is leaning toward you over the steep slope and so very difficult to cross. The alternative, reluctantly recommended, it to turn right on the track, take the first gate on the left, walk up through two fields and cross the aforementioned fence at a point where it allows easy access to open ground above. You may have to evaluate this yourself when you get there. Whatever you do, don't disturb sheep in enclosed fields.

When you reach open ground, however achieved, you may like to relax and admire the view. It's lovely: Lough Anascaul ensconced below surrounding cliffs and above it enticing glimpses of a wider panorama, expanding as you advance.

Rounding crags above and to the left climb by an earthbank cum wall north-west to the highest of the cliffs overlooking Lough Anascaul. Then turn north-east to reach a prominent heap of stones, Cu Chulainn's House. The route from here to the nearby cliff edge overlooking Glanteenassig is simple; follow the line of standing stones (galláin on the map) right to the edge.

From here to near the top of Stradbally Mountain the route is easy to describe: simply keep the cliffs on the right. It's not so easy to walk, since it is uphill most of the way but the views of cliff, lakes and wooded valley are delightful. If for any reason you have to return from along here, simply aim across bogland to reach the top of the track from Glennahoo to Anascaul (say GR 565068 or south of this).

The summit of Stradbally Mountain (798m) is a boulder field and commands lovely views. Prominent among them is the next target, its sister mountain Beenoskee (826m). This is an easy walk on stony ground giving good views over the cliffs of the corrie gouged out between the two mountains. The panorama from Beenoskee, especially towards the Brandon massif, is as good as from Stradbally if not better. Beenoskee has a trig pillar, but one with a lazy disposition, as you will see when you get there.

The target now is the highest point (at GR 565068) on the already mentioned track (hardly more than a rough path where you will meet it). From the summit of Beenoskee aim initially roughly south, avoiding steep ground to the right, to pass a rocky outcrop on the way, a distinct feature in generally nondescript terrain.

Once on the path, head east on a developing track. This takes you initially steeply down between waterfalls and cascades to right and left, and later into remote, scenic level country to Lough Anascaul. A quiet, pleasant end to the day.

ROUTE 9: CAHERCONREE AND BAURTREGAUM

A steady climb along a narrow valley and gorge ends in a remote and impressive Shangri La, a corrie overlooked by cliffs and steep ground. The tough climb from here to the summit of Caherconree reveals a wide panorama, which is sustained for much of the rest of the walk, though the dull underfoot terrain from Caherconree on makes for something of an anti-climax.

Getting There: From Tralee take the N86 for about 7 miles (11km) to cross a hump-backed bridge. Look out just beyond it for a small yellow and black sign bearing the legend 'N86 0071'. Turn next left onto a narrow road (be careful) and park shortly at its end where there is space for 3-4 carefully parked cars (GR 743107). **Buses:** Timetable 273, 275 or 281.

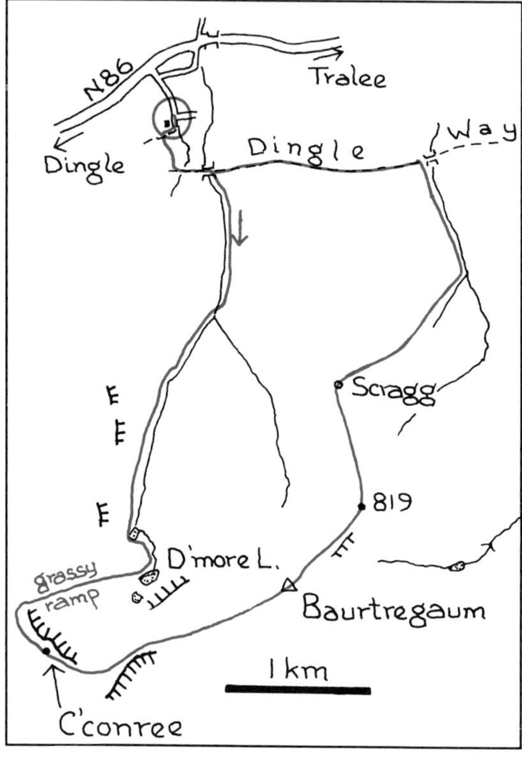

Walking Time: 5 hours (distance 12km, climb 940m).

Difficulties: One steep climb which has to be tackled at the correct point because of cliffs in the area. Some rough ground underfoot.

Map: Sheet 71.

Route: Walk up the road past one house and continue on a path. Cross the nearby second gate on the left and start climbing gently through rough land.

The aim here is the nearby mouth of the gorge of Derrymore River to the south. Before you reach it you will cross the Dingle Way: note this point which will be useful for the return. Once at the mouth you have a choice of west or east bank (east is easier to begin with as there is an outcrop directly on the west bank). It's always that way!

From here on for nearly 3km there's a gentle climb, initially with high vegetation and steep banks underfoot, though it later improves. The route is obvious: follow the stream, ignoring a narrow gorge on the left after about 1km. The hills gradually enfold you, the valley widens into a nearly flat area strewn with the most enormous boulders. At length, and here the valley is again narrower with cliffs on both sides, you will reach the first of three tiny lakes.

From here the second and largest lake, Derrymore Lough, is a short climb through boulders. The easy way to Caherconree from here is to climb a grassy ramp running west. Alternatively, you can walk to the nearby small last lake and climb steeply between the great cliffs guarding the north-east flank of Caherconree.

Caherconree (835m, 2.75 hours) commands excellent views over Dingle and Iveragh. If you have the time it is worth while descending to Caherconree Fort to the south-west, a promontory fort consisting of a stone wall over 100m and 4m thick. It should take about 45 minutes there and back.

So, to Baurtregaum, Caherconree's plain and dumpy sister. Walk east from Caherconree along a short but narrow grassy ridge, a bit too wide and harmless to qualify as a knife edge. From it descend to a wide and sadly eroded col facing Baurtregaum and climb directly to the summit, noting the occasional impressive conglomerate boulder on the way. You should pass a large cairn near the summit plateau; the summit itself (851m) is a little further on at the trig pillar.

The map will suggest several routes from Baurtregaum, none of them really attractive. Walk north-east along a ridge to pt 819m, crowned by a substantial cairn of red stones. On the way you can peer down into the long valley of the Curraheen River on the right. It looks soggy and monotonous but maybe improves on closer acquaintance, which I admit, I haven't accorded it. From pt 819m descend north heading towards Scragg. Just after leaving pt 819m you may meet a short section of steep ground across your route. After it the route is uneventful with Scragg (657m) itself only a point on virtually level ground.

The end of this route is tiring, with lots of high heather underfoot and over-knee, as you wend your weary way north-east towards the valley of Derryquay River. Once you reach the narrow valley walk, or stumble, down keeping to the west of the valley stream where the ground is somewhat easier.

Emerging from the narrow valley you will see a footbridge on the Dingle Way ahead. Turn left onto the Way here and walk less than 2km back to the gorge of Derrymore River where you started. Cross another bridge over the Derrymore, walk another 100m or so and then leave the Way to retrace steps to the start.

Short Variation. Walk as far as Derrymore Lough. This should take about 3 hours there and back. It's a memorable diversion if you are on the Dingle Way. If so, don't mistake the gorge of Derryquay River for the one you want, that of the Derrymore.

Peak Baggers' Variation. A high starting point gives an easy climb to Caherconree. Take the minor road (signed 'Caherconree') running south-east from Camp. Just north of its highest point (at GR 715056) start at the notice board and markers. Walking time is 3 hours (distance 6km, climb 640m.)

ROUTE 10: CONNOR PASS TO BEENBO

An A to B route which encompasses some of the wildest and most remote terrain in Dingle, as well as some of the best views. Starting high above the great corries east of Connor Pass, the route descends steeply into a country of rocky outcrops, lochans and small but steep-sided peaks.

Getting There: Park one car at the start at Connor Pass carpark (GR 4905), about 4 miles (6km) north-east of Dingle and about 22 miles (35km) from Tralee.

Park the other car on the side of the road at or about a former national school on the south of Connor Hill Road at GR 541103. This point is about 4½ miles (7.5km) from the Pass. If you are coming from the Tralee direction you should start watching out when you reach a distinct U-turn in the road.

Walking Time: 4.75 hours (distance 10km, climb 620m). This allows about 1 hour extra for a considerable 960m of descent, including one very steep section.
Difficulties: Navigation is simple as far as pt 670m (GR 515063), the point of last return. After this, as well as a steep, tiring descent, good navigation is needed in an area with few distinct features and several areas of cliffs. If all else fails, head east to the track running from Glennahoo to Anascaul (see also under route 7).
Map: Sheet 70.
Route: From the carpark head south-east along a track but leave it after a hundred metres or so to keep to the edge of the cliffs overlooking Connor Hill Road. For the next two kilometres navigation is easy and the views down into corries and their lakes are delightful. A stone shelter presages the one summit on this stretch, Slievanea (over 620m). The shelter is a useful landmark in bad weather because the summit itself barely rises above the general level and, wedged between two corries and so a little off the direct line, can be missed, though it doesn't matter too much if it is.

After Slievanea the cliffs tend to soften and swing to the north-east. Still following their edge, walk to pt 670m (no cairn). This summit, it is hardly necessary to say, is an excellent viewpoint. It is also both the point of last return and the point of departure for the Anascaul variation (see below).

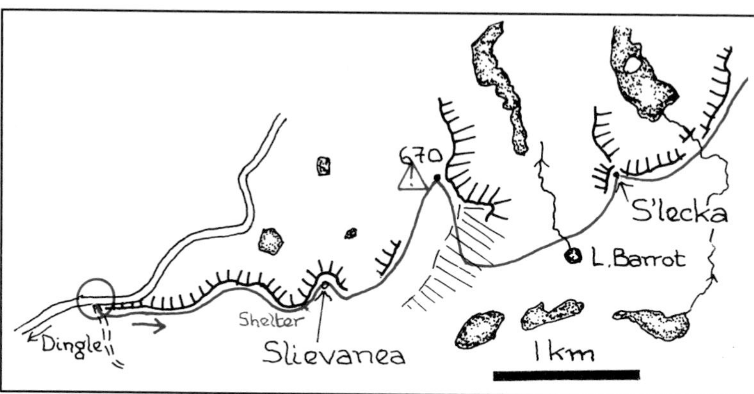

Things are a lot sterner from here on. In good weather you might follow the cliff edge south-east for a short distance for the views (in bad weather head directly south from the summit). Beware especially of one section of this cliff: as you will see from the sketch map it appears to offer a route down to the east. It doesn't; instead it ends on a rocky and dangerous promontory. However, before you reach this promontory you will probably have had to veer sharply away from the cliff edge (so heading almost south) to descend steeply over grass.

A good time to contemplate the next section of the route is at the foot of this steep ground. Beyond the rocky hummocks ahead the three next peaks are easy climbs from this side (only); they are all about the same height; they are all backed by a soggy area of bogland beyond which is an undulating line of mountains; all offering varied views over small corries and towards the coastal plain.

So, first cross the outlet stream from Lough Barrot, then swing north to climb Slievenalecka (456m). Keeping cliffs on the left cross a stream which is quickening for a splendid cascade into Loch an Dúin and then climb Slievegower (484m). This leaves only Beenbo (474m).

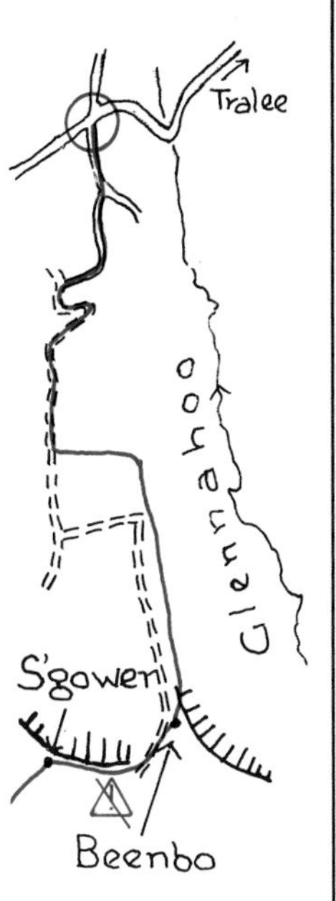

Beenbo is now unmistakable. Formerly it was a fine grassy peak with a long spur heading north which offered fine views down into Glennahoo. It still gives those views but summit and spur have been brutally raped by an agricultural road hacked almost along the crest of the spur.

Walk the road for a short distance, then climb to the summit and make your way down and north, keeping to the right of the crest to avoid the sight of the road. After a rocky section on the crest continue over pt 298m and then drop west to meet a track (an ordinary track). Keep on this track, choosing the 'main' option where a choice has to be made, and you will reach Connor Hill Road. Depending on where you parked, turn right or left for the car.

Anascaul Variation: Not so interesting as the main route but may be more convenient if you are staying in Dingle, especially as there is a good bus service from Anascaul.

From pt 670m head south-west, so that you are initially practically backtracking, walk to the col facing Croaghskearda (606m) and climb to the summit. From here on simply walk east for 7km along an undulating line of mountains with only one severe dip, that to Windy Gap (GR 5304). When you reach the cairn (at GR 572050) close to the cliffs overlooking Lough Anascaul, you can descend south-east to the road (an easy but not so scenic route). Alternatively you can descend steeply on grass north-west, cross one (maybe two) streams set in deep gorges, and then swing right over fairly steep ground to reach a track north of a shed. This is a more scenic route giving excellent views of the lake, but best walked on a clear day. (See also the sketch map under route 8.) In either case walk into Anascaul. Walking time 6.25 hours (distance from Connor Pass 16km, climb 650m), including 1 hour for steep descents. This may be considerably reduced if pt 670m is by-passed.

ROUTE 11: CIRCUIT OF GLANTEENASSIG

A fairly undemanding gradual climb up the rock-strewn eastern shoulder of Stradbally Mountain (798m), with its great red sandstone cliffs and buttresses increasingly dominant. The descent follows the top of the cliffs above the lakes and wooded areas of Glanteenassig and its sub-valleys, before descending around sandstone cliffs south of Lough Slat. A varied and memorable walk.

Getting There: From Tralee (16 miles (26km) away) take the N86, keep straight ahead on the R560 where the N86 swings left, keep straight ahead again where the R560 swings right for Castlegregory, then take the next turn left after only a few hundred metres (it is at present (1996) signed 'Glass Studio'). Drive another 1.3 miles (2.1km) to park carefully on the verge (GR 618099). Alternatively, you can park a little further on to shorten the road walk at the end. From Connor Hill Road direction watch out for the sign for the glass studio or return from the R560 if you overshoot the right turn. **Buses:** Timetable 273 to the junction for Castlegregory (GR 6211).

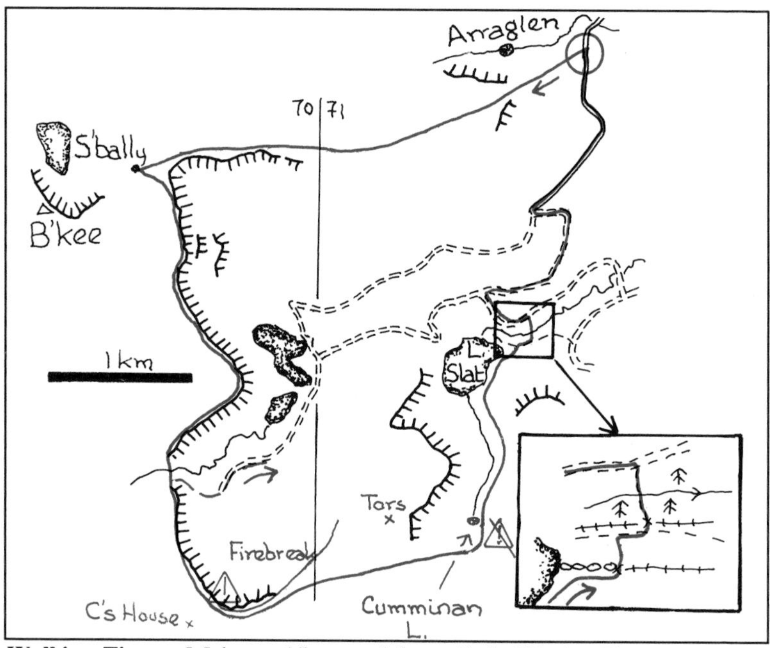

Walking Time: 5.5 hours (distance 14km, climb 980m). There are several opportunities, both easier and harder, to vary this.

Difficulties: Easy underfoot and navigationally, except on the last descent where attention to navigation is necessary.

Map: Sheets 70 and 71. Sheet 70 in particular shows forest well in excess of reality.

Route: From the start, as well as picking out much of the circuit, you will observe near at hand the spur south of Arraglen Lake, which is to be climbed first, and whose difficult, rocky terrain is not a foretaste of what is to come! You can clamber over boulders on the crest if you are so inclined; however it is probably easier to walk along the lakeshore or on the right of the crest of the spur, which gives lovely views down into the corrie holding the lake.

After a short distance the slope eases and a long, steady climb westward to the summit of Stradbally Mountain ensues. As you advance the cliffs on the left become more formidable, though not as formidable as the cliffs off to the south of Stradbally. Here massive, almost vertical slabs, a mighty buttress and scree spilling downwards towards the wooded shores of Lough Cam far below make a dramatic scene.

An increasing number of rocks heralds the summit of Stradbally Mountain (798m). In fact the summit itself, crowned by a huge cairn, is a boulder field. The forest shown on sheet 70 reaching to the summit is nowhere near it, which is just as well because the views from here, close to the centre of the peninsula, are magnificent and only a little impaired by Stradbally's twin, nearby Beenoskee.

If you are into peak-bagging you might like to climb Beenoskee (826m), whose summit is obvious because of its toppled trig pillar. If you do make sure you reach the next section of cliff south of Stradbally as high on the shoulder of that mountain as possible; otherwise you will miss some of the best scenery.

From Stradbally walk south-east to the nearby cliffs and simply follow them down, keeping them on the left. A lovely section, giving new angles on the cliffs and down into the woods and lakes of Glanteenassig, the centre-piece of the walk.

After nearly 2km from the summit of Stradbally, the slope eases and the cliff edge swings decisively from south-east to south-west. Beyond this, and here the cliff swings back to south-west, you may like to avail of an escape route (at 3 hours' walking time). Watch out where forest creeps up what is now merely steep ground on the left. Here you can clamber down the grassy slope to the valley floor and then follow a stream to the nearby forest track.

If however you wish to do the whole route, continue along the cliff edge, noting as you once again reach nearly level ground a huge mound of stones off to the right. This is locally known as Cu Chulainn's house (see notes under route 8).

Navigation is now the main priority. In bad weather, with the map sheets' boundary to worry about as well as everything else, simply walk along the cliff edge until it swings north-east and then follow a compass bearing of 77° for 2km - this should take you to the spur just south of Cumminan Lough (see below). In good weather you can afford to follow a line of red stones along the crest of the spur. This is not part of an old roadway; instead, more prosaically it is a firebreak, though in spite of the map's assertion otherwise, the nearest forest is a long way down the slope. Follow this firebreak round to the north-east to pt 541m. Beyond it, where the firebreak descends to the left, keep to the crest of a now broad ridge.

There are two prominent tors (heaps of rocks) to the north of the rounded summit of pt 552m. To avoid cliffs to the east of the summit you should steer well to its south so as to walk to just south of Cumminan Lough and then turn directly to the lough itself.

Navigational troubles now behind, walk north to descend a fairly steep, grassy slope to the shores of Lough Slat. It's a lovely location: the large lake set in an isolated bowl, a partly wooded lakeside and high, frowning slabs of cliff soaring above to west and south-east.

A complicated set of directions now follows that take you only a few hundred metres. Please bear with me and don't quote it as typical of my writing style!

Turn right when you reach the lakeshore and right again away from the lake at a high stone wall, which ends only 100m or so from the lake at a gate. Cross this gate to reach a path bordering forest and turn right onto it. Cross the first gate on the left into forest and ford the river. Walk to a track and turn left. Walk to a tee and turn right. Now simply keep to this one and only track until you are out of forest. Turn right onto a minor road and walk less than 2km to the start.

Longer Variations. When you reach the spur south of Cumminan Lough you can climb Doon and descend to the valley of the Drishoge River or you can climb Knocknakilton and Cummeen and descend by Lough Acummeen.

On the Slopes of Crohane (Route 15)

EAST IVERAGH

East Iveragh consists of the large area to the east of Lough Caragh (known to one and all - except the OS - as Caragh Lake) and the road through Ballaghbeama Gap. At the east is Mangerton (routes 12, 14, 16) and its satellites. Mangerton itself (839m) has a flat, boggy summit but its magnificent northern corries make up for this deficiency. Close by is the lower hill country south and south-east of Lough Guitane which, although it rises to only 656m, is a fascinatingly varied area, which belies its modest stature (route 15).

South-west of Killarney is the lofty (757m) Purple Mountain group, an area of easy walking (route 18). It is bound on the west by the great defile of the Gap of Dunloe (route 19). Westward again is the 6-km long Reeks Ridge, which has some of the highest peaks in Ireland, as well as splendid corries, those on its northern side being especially good (routes 19, 21, 22). The Ridge terminates on the great horseshoe of peaks surrounding Coomloughra, which boasts Ireland's three highest mountains, namely Caher, Carrauntoohil and Beenkeragh, the latter two linked by the knife-edge of the Beenkeragh Ridge (routes 20, 21).

The two east-west ranges south of the Reeks (routes 13, 17, 23), of which the imposing but dull Broaghnabinnia (745m) is the highest summit, are dwarfed by the Reeks, but give good walking and excellent views.

ROUTE 12: OLD KENMARE ROAD

An easy walk on path, track and side road (and alas, main road) through moorland and an old oak forest, one of the very few in Ireland which might be primeval.

Getting There: If you have no car you can start in Killarney and walk the Kerry Way to the carpark at the foot of Torc Waterfall (GR 966848), a distance of 7km, nearly half of which is on road. You can time your arrival at Derrycunihy Church (GR 914803) to meet the timetable 280 bus into Killarney and so avoid the walk on the main road.

By car from Killarney on the N71, park at the carpark on the left close to the foot of Torc Waterfall (GR 966848), about 4 miles (6km) south of the town.

Walking Time: Starting and finishing at Torc Waterfall carpark should take about 5.5 hours (distance 22km, climb 360m).

Difficulties: The main danger is that of being struck by a car on the N71. Generally easy underfoot conditions permit fast progress.

Map: A wide choice. Sheet 78, 1:25 000 "Killarney National Park" or the National Park one-inch map are equally acceptable.

Route: From the carpark take the Kerry Way alongside Torc Waterfall, well-known more because of its accessibility than its inherently wild and dramatic qualities. At its top continue on the Way into moorland south of Torc Mountain and then over a quaking area around Crinnagh River. The route continues gently upward and then equally gently downward through an old oak forest whose trees and surrounds are home to prodigious volumes of moss.

Beyond the forest the Way divides, the left fork heading for Kenmare and the right, the one you take, heading for the N71 at Derrycunihy Church. On the N71 turn right and follow it generally downhill for a considerable 7km on a winding road which carries a comparatively heavy load of traffic.

It will therefore be with some relief that you eventually turn left onto a narrow tarred road, the first since reaching the N71. This you can follow through

Muckross Estate, over wooded islands linked by bridges, and along narrow peninsulas to Muckross House itself. No detailed directions are required as the way is obvious, well signposted and there are always lots of people around to ask if in doubt.

ROUTE 13: THE BLACK VALLEY

Except for a short section which is muddy and rocky underfoot, a gentle stroll first along the Kerry Way and then on minor roads, with wild and remote mountains rising in all directions.

Getting There: The route starts from Black Valley youth hostel (GR 8682) though it may be adapted for those starting in the Glencar area, for which the modifications may be found under route 23.

Walking Time: 2.5 hours (distance 12km, climb 100m).

Difficulties: Wellies recommended because of the wet stretch through forest. Otherwise easy underfoot and no navigational problems.

Map: None needed.

Route: As described in route 22, take the Kerry Way till it meets the end of a rough road after 5km (say a little over an hour's walking). Turn left onto this road and follow it past two lakes back to the Kerry Way. Turn right for the start.

ROUTE 14: MANGERTON

An overlong track leads to superb views over the Devil's Punch Bowl and down into the L-shaped Horses' Glen. Behind the rim of the Horses' Glen hides the boggy plateau of Mangerton (839m), so this is a route treading the narrow line between memorable terrain and dull.

Getting There: The start (at GR 983848) is about 5 miles (8km) from Killarney. From the town take the N71, turning left off it after about 2½ miles (4km) (signposted reassuringly 'Mangerton 2¾'). After 1 mile turn right (it's on a corner) also signposted for Mangerton. Drive onward for a little over a mile (about 2km) to park at or near a concrete bridge on the left. There is plenty of room for parking here. If you reach Junction D (see page 3) which has a sign for Mangerton, you are nonetheless too far east.

Walking Time: 5 hours (distance 14km, climb 780m) including a little time for a steep descent - counterbalanced by some easy track walking.

Difficulties: The Mangerton plateau is wet and peat-haggy. The steep descent from Stoompa and the last trek across bogland may prove time-consuming. Navigation is easy, though in bad weather it is advisable to avoid the summit of Mangerton, which adds little to the walk and makes the navigation more difficult.

Map: Sheets 78 and 79, with most on sheet 78. "Killarney National Park" (1:25 000) covers the same ground as sheet 78.

Route: Cross the concrete bridge and take the rough track beyond all the way south to the Devil's Punch Bowl, a corrie lake. The track is easy enough to follow, being straight and relentlessly uphill for much of the way, though near the Bowl it veers right to traverse a shoulder.

The first sight of the lake is from a lovely location: high above it on the rocky moraine at its north-eastern side. At 1.75 hours walking time this is a good place for a break and the point to turn back if you want only a short walk.

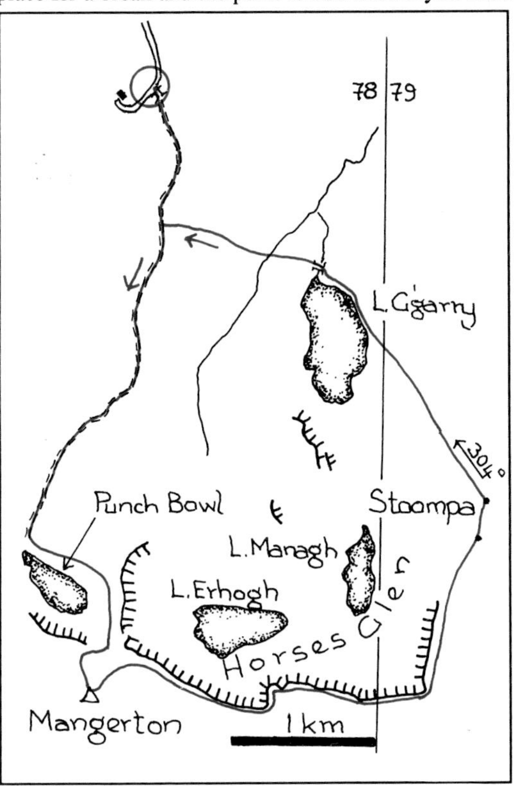

Beyond the Bowl you will see the Mangerton plateau stretching away to the east, with an obvious ramp leading to it rising from the lake's left. It is a short but steep climb to the plateau, the Bowl on the right and the Horses' Glen on the left. If the weather is clear and you are intent on bagging peaks you might like to cross the peat hags to reach the summit of Mangerton (839m) a few hundred metres away. Mangerton's main interest is that it is the most uninteresting summit in Ireland: its only distinguishing feature is its trig pillar - and an arrow formed of stones indicating the way back. (You can't take it with you.)

Back at the plateau edge head roughly east, Lough Erhogh far below. This is a truly delightful stretch: the steep sides of the huge corrie immediately on the left, a marvellous array of peaks including the Reeks and perhaps far-off Brandon. After 2km or so the cliff edge turns abruptly at right-angles north. Continue along the edge, Lough Managh now far below, to climb north to the flattish top of twinned-topped Stoompa (705m, 3.75 hours), the only distinct peak of the day.

From Stoompa continue north steeply downward to reach the shore of broad Lough Garagarry, navigation not helped by the unfortunate cross-over from sheet 79 to 78 (a compass bearing of 304° or a little less from the northern summit of Stoompa will get you to the lakeshore). Once there walk along the shore and cross the outlet stream on a neat bridge a hundred or so metres from the lake. From here you must reach the nearest point of the outward track about 1km away to the west. Once on it turn right for the nearby start.

ROUTE 15: BENNAUNMORE

A small, quite low area (Bennaunmore is only 454m, though Crohane at the edge of the area reaches 656m) but one of constantly changing atmosphere and with a wealth of small-scale features, some a legacy of former volcanic activity. Essentially this an area for leisurely pottering: or at least *slow* pottering, given the difficult terrain underfoot.

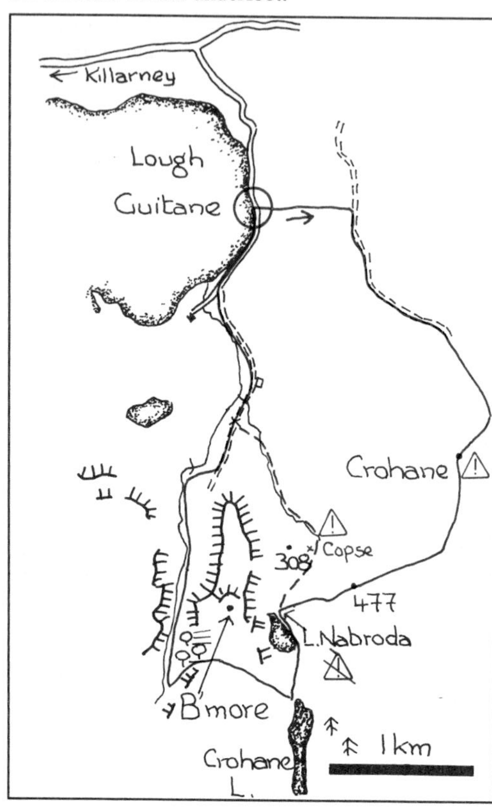

Getting There: The start is about 8 miles (13km) from Killarney. Take the N71, turn left off it after about 2½ miles (4km) just after Muckross Park Hotel - the turn is signposted 'Mangerton 2¾'. Continue straight ahead to cross the bridge at Junction D (see page 3), drive 1.8 miles (2.9km) along the length of Lough Guitane and take the next turn right (it's narrow and has gate pillars). Drive a further 0.7 miles (1.1km) and park just after a farmhouse on the right, at a point where there is a linear quarry on the left (GR 036846). This point may also be easily reached from the N22. If you want to do the short variation the starting point is a little further on where the road swings right to a farmhouse and a track branches left (GR 033840). Considerate parking should not be difficult along the road.

Walking Time: 4.75 hours, thus allowing about 1 hour for difficult terrain (distance 10km, climb 720m).

Difficulties: Much treacherous ground. One stretch needs attention to navigation.

Map: Sheet 79.

Route: The first few hundred metres are the worst in the whole route, so let's get them over with. Climb the quarry on the left of the road and continue upward heading east, praying that you will soon meet a track running south (it is not shown on the current sheet 79). This is extremely difficult ground with high vegetation and low rocks, just great for crocking an ankle. As you climb the going gets easier, but still you will no doubt be relieved to reach the track and turn right onto it to face Crohane.

The track winds upward to flat ground on Crohane's northern spur, giving widening views of the rugged area to the west and of the well-named Paps off to the east. The end of the track still leaves a stiff climb to the eastern summit, leaving a short walk to the north-facing crags on the summit itself (656m, 2 hours).

The descent from Crohane requires careful navigation as the country to the south-west is rough with no distinct features. First walk south, then veer west to climb pt 477m. The next target is the northern end of Lough Nabroda, which requires a careful descent because of steep ground and the occasional rocky outcrop. As you descend you can study the great columns of rock on the eastern side of Bennaunmore, evidence of its volcanic origin.

Lough Nabroda is in a dramatic location, steeply rising ground close by to east and west accentuating its remoteness. Incidentally there is no evident outlet stream - it runs underground through huge boulders on the lake's northern end. The lakeshore is an excellent place for a rest, after which you should take a path south along the lake's eastern side. Where it expires continue to the northern end of Crohane Lake at which, in spite of sheet 79's assertion to the contrary, there is only a straggle of trees set back from the shore.

If you have plenty of time you might like to wander (or more accurately struggle - this is tough terrain) along the western shore of Crohane Lake. However the route proper continues to the col to the west, south of the highest Bennaunmore (454m). To avoid unnecessary climbing a bearing from the lake might be useful. At this col you may like to consider a there-and-back to Bennaunmore - after all, it does give the route its title. Then make a short, steep, tough descent westward through ancient oaks to the floor of Cappagh Glen. This is a lovely stretch: trees clothing the slopes on both sides of the narrow defile with the stern crags of Eskduff close by on the other side.

Turn right on the valley floor and follow the stream, keeping the main river on the left. This is a pleasant walk and an easy one, except for the occasional heaps of boulders to climb. Clamber through a narrow gap between cliffs into more open country. Continue to follow the stream until it swings decisively right. Here look out for a track a little higher up on the right on the lower slopes of Bennaunmore. Walk to it and follow it roughly north (it's indistinct in places) to cross a gate. Continue north on what is now a good track, the main stream still on the left, past an abandoned house and onto tarmac. The start is only a few hundred metres further on along the shore.

Easy Variation. A shorter distance certainly (walking time is 3.5 hours (distance 7km, climb 340m)), but with an even greater proportion of tough terrain. From the parking place follow the left track, that is the one which does not lead to the farm. As you advance initially south-east you will see rumpled Bennaunmore near at hand and to its left, a smaller version, pt 308m.

Follow the track past a derelict house, cross a gate and then walk south-east to and along the valley's stream to the left of pt. 308m. This is rough ground which ends near the source of the stream at a tiny level patch with a copse sheltering under a rocky buttress on the right. From here a compass bearing of about 190° will take you to Lough Nabroda and the main route.

Very Easy Variation. Walk the end of the main route by entering the Cappagh Glen to the right of Bennaunmore. Return by the same route.

ROUTE 16: PEAKEEN AND KNOCKANAGUISH

A high valley with touches of Switzerland about it, followed by two low (509m and 555m) but tough climbs through crags. A short route which can be easily varied, and an interesting diversion from the Kerry Way.

Getting There: From Kenmare take the road past the hospital (it's also the Kerry Way) and continue straight ahead for 2.7 miles (4.3km) to a cross roads. Park carefully (GR 917752). **Bus:** Timetables 270, 282 to Kenmare; timetable 280 at Derrycunihy Church for the variation from the north.

Walking Time: 4 hours (distance 9km, climb 620m), including an extra half-hour for one craggy descent.

Difficulties: Not as easy as its short length would suggest. The crags on the descent from Knockanaguish require some care (or a diversion) and there is much rough ground.

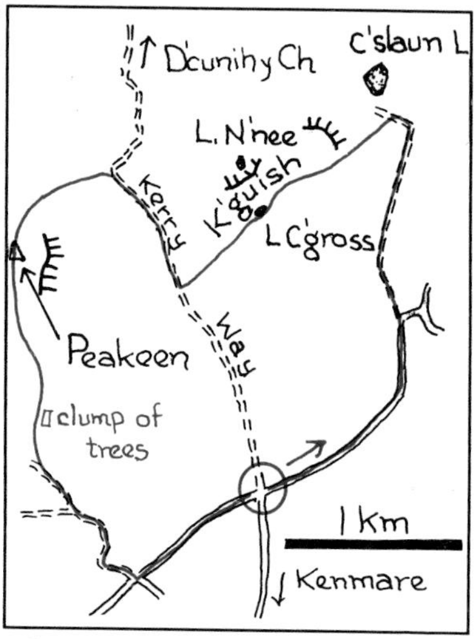

Map: Sheet 78.

Route: Walk east along the road on a gradual uphill. After about 1km the road swings north and gradually assumes track status, simultaneously entering a scenic valley with the rugged slopes of Knockanaguish on one side, trees decorously clothing rocky slopes on the other.

At the highest point on the track and with Cummeenslaun Lake ahead fronting undulating ground, climb steeply south-west to Knockanaguish (509m), keeping cliffs to the right.

Knockanaguish has a set of rocky hummocks on its indeterminate summit plateau, so perhaps the best place to consider the next move is to walk on to Lough Cummeenagross at its far (south-western) side. The problem now is to get off the summit. You can cautiously work your way down to Lough Nagannee to the north-west avoiding some unfriendly crags en route. However, perhaps the safest way is to head south-west from Lough Cummeenagross, veering left if trouble threatens. This will take you down to the Kerry Way just south of a rocky spur, where if you turn left you can reach the start in less than a half-hour. If you want to climb Peakeen turn right and walk the short distance (and not so short climb) to reach the top of the track. From here keep cliffs on the left to climb steeply, avoiding (or climbing) a formidable set of slabs just north of the summit to reach the trig pillar (555m).

From the summit head south initially and when you see a dense clump of trees below veer left over upland fields to reach it. Walk onward downhill to a house a few hundred metres away, where you can pick up a track. Take this track down to a nearby tee, turn left and left again onto tarmac for the nearby start.

Variations. You could start in Kenmare, a pleasant walk all on the Kerry Way. If you are staying to the north of the area, you could walk from Derrycunihy Church (GR 9180), take the Kerry Way and climb the two peaks from there.

Take care to retrace your steps carefully from Peakeen. You can also extend the walk onto high, rough country to the west of Peakeen.

ROUTE 17: KNOCKLOMENA

With higher and more impressive peaks to north and west, the line of mountains running from Knocklomena to Boughil is a little overshadowed. Nonetheless it makes an enjoyable walk: a narrow rocky range reaching only 641m, with stretches of impressive cliffs on one side and marvellous views of high peaks in most directions.

Getting There: From Killarney (18 miles, 29km to GR 807780) take the N71 to Moll's Gap, turn right onto the R568 here and shortly first right. If you have two cars leave one at this junction (GR 853774), drive the other onward to a tee, turn left and drive along the narrow road for a further 2.2 miles (3.5km) to a grassy area on the right where three (not more) cars may be parked (GR 807780). If you have only one car you can park anywhere along the road forming part of the route.

This point may also be easily reached from Kenmare (10 miles (16km)) or from Black Valley youth hostel. **Bus:** Timetable 280 bus from Moll's Gap or the R568.

Walking Time: 4.25 hours for the A to B route (distance 9km, climb 920m), with an additional 1.25 hours for the 6km road walk if you haven't a second car.

Difficulties: Some very wet ground near the start. Navigation generally easy though there are stretches of cliff to avoid and none of the summits has a prominent cairn.

Map: Sheet 78 or 1:25 000 "Macgillycuddy's Reeks".

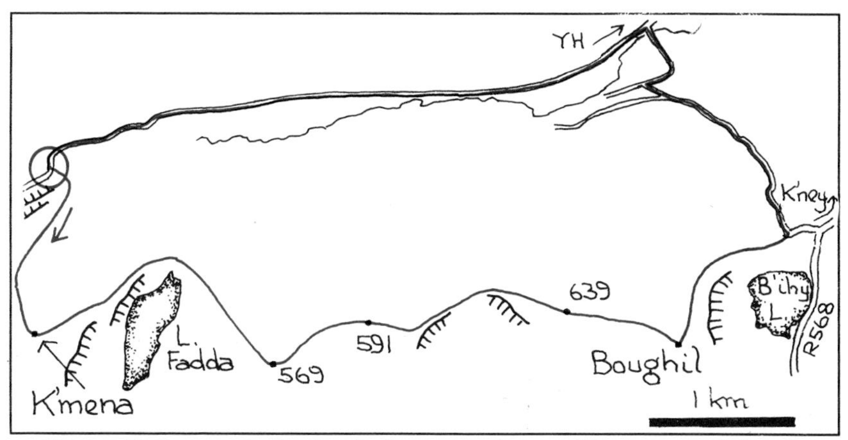

Route: Walk onward a few hundred metres to the top of the pass, turn left at the stile here and follow a fence upward and south-west to its upper end where a rocky outcrop marks the summit of Knocklomena (641m). This is a great viewing point with the mighty line of mountains culminating in the pyramid of Mullaghanattin prominent to the west. Incidentally the pointed peak to the east and comparatively close at hand is pt 639m, the second-last peak to be climbed. Descend north-east to avoid cliffs to the east and so reach a very wet area just to the north of Lough Fadda. From here it is a tough climb to 569m.

The next section (to pt 639m) is the most satisfying of the whole route: a narrow rocky ridge, steep ground and cliffs to the south, with a steep descent and ascent between pts 595m and 639m. One navigational aid in bad visibility: there is a fence or boundary stones most of the way from pt 569m to pt 639m, about 2km away.

From pt 639m continue east to Boughil (631m) where further eastward progress is abruptly terminated by cliffs. Turn north to avoid them and then swing gradually right to pass north of Barfinnihy Lough. This is difficult, tiring descent necessitating many detours to avoid slabs. If you are bound for the starting point you should veer left to the road. If not, perhaps the best option is to cross the flat mound north of Barfinnihy Lough and so reach the road close to the junction where the car is parked.

ROUTE 18: PURPLE MOUNTAIN GROUP

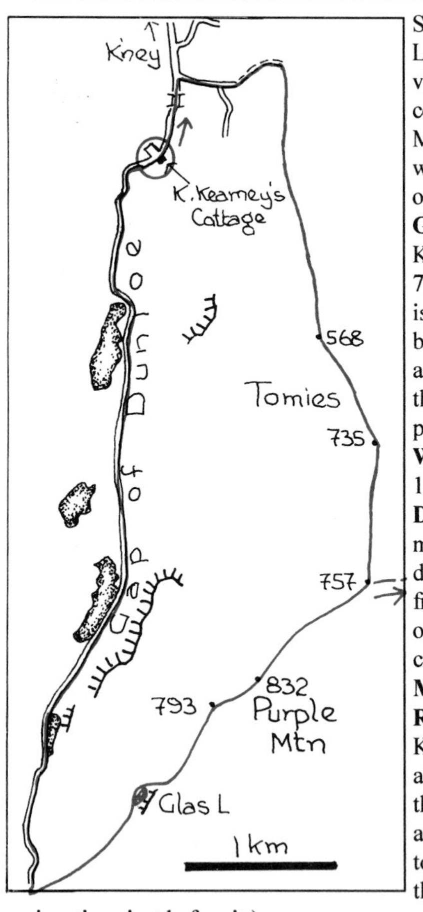

Situated between the Reeks and the Lakes of Killarney and offering good views of each, the heather-covered and com-paratively gently sloped Purple Mountain Group (832m) gives easy walking though without the excitement of the more rugged Reeks.

Getting There: The start, Kate Kearney's Cottage (GR 8888), is about 7½ miles (12km) from Killarney. There is ample parking. **Bus:** take timetable bus 14 or 42 (both express) or 279 to and from Beaufort Bridge (GR 8892), thus leaving a walk of 4km to the start proper.

Walking Time: 5.5 hours (distance 14km, climb 900m).

Difficulties: Underfoot conditions are mostly good and navigation easy with distinct tops. Beware of a direct descent from Purple Mountain itself to the Gap of Dunloe: there are numerous cliffs and crags on the way.

Map: Sheet 78 or either 1:25,000 map.

Route: From the large carpark at Kate Kearney's Cottage, walk north back along the road, cross a bridge after less than 400m and turn next right. (If you are on the bus you don't of course have to go as far as the Cottage - turn left at the second of two closely spaced junctions just before it.)

Ignoring a turn on the right, continue straight ahead on what soon becomes a track. Cross a gate at its end and beyond it follow a path which swings right onto the northern spur of Tomies Mountain (568m), one of several tops loosely designated as such on the map. From here it is a stiff climb to the highest Tomies (735m, 2.5 hours), which is marked by various stone edifices.

The route continues south to pt 757m, where you have to make a decision whether to swing generally north-east, take in Shehy Mountain and thence follow forest tracks back to the start. If you have already been in the Gap of Dunloe this is the way to go; since it is easy navigationally, there is no need to describe the route. If you want to do the main route climb Purple Mountain (832m) to the south-west, the highest point of the day and a lovely viewpoint.

From Purple Mountain head down to Glas Lough, a useful landmark though not essential to find, where you should watch out for crags to its east. From there you can reach the Head of the Gap (GR 871837). The return route takes in the entire length of the Gap, an impressive defile 5km long with beetling crags and cliffs pressing in on both sides for much of the way. However as you walk northwards back to Kate Kearney's Cottage the scenery gets tamer, the valley widens out and the numbers of day-trippers increase. By the time you get to the Cottage you will probably feel that the Gap could do with being a little shorter or the crowds a little less evident.

Much Longer Variation. You can combine this route with route 19 to give a walking time of 7 hours (distance 16km, climb 1450m).

A(ghadoe) to B(lack Valley) Variation. If you are staying in youth hostels you can walk between the hostels at Aghadoe (near Killarney) and Black Valley, thus making an attractive A to B walk.

The start of the route is obvious from the map (note that part of the way is the same as that for travellers by bus given above). When you reach the road at the Head of the Gap, turn left and walk down to the hostel. Walking time is 6 hours (distance 17km, climb 820m).

This route can of course also be done in reverse to get from Black Valley to Aghadoe hostel.

ROUTE 19: THE EASTERN REEKS

Emphatically not the most exciting section of the Reeks, though still a good walk with the possibility of an extension into more rugged terrain to the west.

Getting There: The starting point is at Kate Kearney's Cottage (GR 8888), reached as described in route 18.

Walking Time: 5 hours (distance 14km, climb 750m). The variation is about 2 hours longer.

Difficulties: Some indistinct terrain which requires careful navigation, especially as this is the one area where there are a few crags. Underfoot generally good except for some wet ground near the end.

Map: Sheet 78 or 1:25 000 "Macgillycuddy's Reeks".

Route: Evading the entreaties of the jarveymen, walk south on tarmac into the Gap of Dunloe, an impressive defile with cliffs on both sides and a few scenic lakes on the narrow floor. Just after a few zig-zags the ground levels off and the real walking begins (1.75 hours).

The goal now is Drishana (464m), reached by climbing steeply from the right of the road, evading crags as you progress. This may throw you a little off course but the general intention is clear: to reach high ground nearby to the west and then swing north with it to the summit, which is noticeable only in retrospect because of the slight drop after it. However the way ahead, uphill through rough and undulating country is clear, though a spot of compass work wouldn't go amiss.

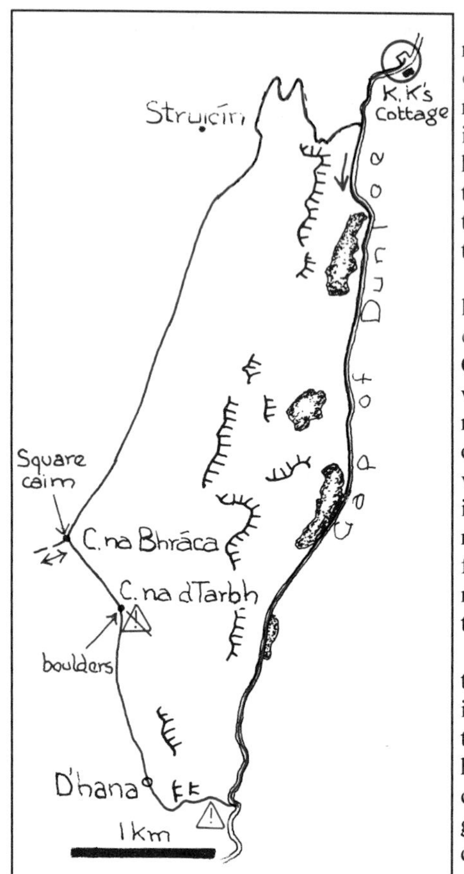

Cnoc na dTarbh (655m) is the next target, and the heaps of enormous boulders on its summit may be reassuring navigationally in bad visibility. The views from here are quite good with part of the Reeks Ridge on one side and the Purple Mountain group on the other.

A moderately steep descent and longer ascent takes you to the distinctive square-cut cairn on Cnoc an Bhráca and a decision: whether to extend the walk into much more memorable territory on the Reeks Ridge (see the variation). If you decide against it the rest is easy: simply push north over a dreary plain heading for, but not climbing, the slight rise of Struicán (440m) 3km off to the north.

A path starts on the plateau just to the south-east of Struicán. It is important to find it because the alternative, a wade through high vegetation, is too awful to contemplate. The path gives good views over the trees, lakes, cliff and crags on the northern end of the Gap before reaching tarmac, the same tarmac you toiled up earlier in the day. Turn left for the nearby start.

Long Variation. From Cnoc an Bhráca walk west to the col overlooking Loch an Chaca, then take the increasing rocky and narrow ridge to the grotto on Cruach Mhór (932m). Return by the same route. The extra walking time is 2 hours, allowing some time for slow going on the narrow ridge.

Note

There's a lot to be said for walking this route in the opposite direction, since you are then facing into a scenic section of the Reeks Ridge on the plateau south of Struicán. However, it does make the navigation more difficult on the descent to the road.

ROUTE 20: THE BEENKERAGH RIDGE

A moderately short but tough walk which takes in the three highest peaks in Ireland, passing from Carrauntoohil (1039m) to Beenkeragh (1010m) along the finest (and most vertigo-inducing) ridge walk in Ireland, the Beenkeragh Ridge. Predictably marvellous views. All in all, a classic, but if you suffer from vertigo, don't attempt it.

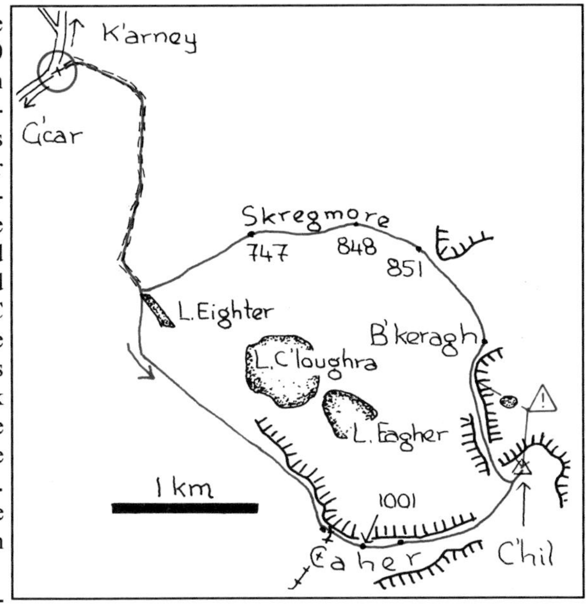

Getting There: The start is roughly 20 miles (32km) from Killarney via Killorglin, though there is a shorter but slower route through Beaufort. In Killorglin take the road signposted 'Glencar 15km' and turn right at junction C (see page 2). Continue onward for 1.2 miles (1.9km) to park carefully at or before double gates on the left (GR 772870). This point may also be easily reached from the Glencar direction.

Walking (and Scrambling) Time: 6.75 hours, including about one hour for scrambling (distance 12km, climb 1260m).

Difficulties: The vertigo-inducing potential of this route has already been alluded to. If you walk the route in the anti-clockwise direction as suggested here, you will face the worst part of the Beenkeragh Ridge first and so you can retreat if needs be, having declined the challenge, but with Carrauntoohil climbed. Navigation is easy and underfoot conditions good.

Map: The 1:25 000 "Macgillycuddy's Reeks" map shows the Beenkeragh ridge clearly; the alternative, sheet 78 is too cramped to do so. However, there is no mistaking the ridge, so perhaps its poor depiction on sheet 78 doesn't matter.

Route: From the gates follow the track all the way to its end at a dam at the western end of Lough Eighter (don't confuse it with Lough Eagher, further east). The dull stretch now behind, walk south to reach a long spur heading towards the summit of Caher, and on the spur's crest turn south-east to follow an increasingly clear path upward to Caher, the huge cliffs overlooking Lough Eagher increasingly imposing on the left.

Caher (1001m) is in effect a long, narrow, grassy ridge, with three summits (the crossways fence between the first and second maybe some help in bad visibility). From the third summit, there is a distinct drop before the final climb to Carrauntoohil itself.

At 1039m, Carrauntoohil is the highest mountain in Ireland and has a fitting location. A blunt wedge pointing north, it is faced on the north and east by formidable cliffs, while to the north-east runs the jagged Beenkeragh ridge, to which we must now address ourselves.

It is most important to retrace steps less than 100m south-west from the summit so as to face the ridge squarely; it initially runs north-west. That done you have to find your way along the narrow rocky ground where, as already said, the most 'airy' part comes early on, after a col south of a Cumeenoughter Lake (GR 8480). To avoid the worst, look out for traces of a path on the left (west) of the crest.

The definitive end of the Ridge is heralded by a steep rock-strewn ascent to Beenkeragh (1010m), from where take the north-west (not north-east) ridge on an exhilarating jaunt over the three main summits of Skregmore.

The end of the Skregmore summits is obvious: there is a steep descent to Lough Eighter. From here pick up the outward track back to the start.

ROUTE 21: CARRAUNTOOHIL FROM HAG'S GLEN

The Hag's Glen is well known: a narrow valley with curious rock pillars on one side and two large scenic lakes at its end. From here the route climbs steeply through tiny, delectable valleys on the Glen's western side to reach Carrauntoohil. The return takes in a section of the Reeks Ridge. A lovely, memorable walk.

Getting There: From Killarney drive to Beaufort, then take the road which skirts the northern side of the Reeks, turning left just after Kissane's shop at the sign 'Carrauntoohil 4'. Drive to the end of the road and park in the carpark (GR 837873), where there is a small charge. This point may also be reached from Killorglin by taking the road signed 'Glencar 15km' in the village, turning left at Junction C (see page 2) and right at the sign 'Carrauntoohil 4'.

Walking Time: 7.75 hours (distance 18km, climb 1350m) but with an option to shorten (see below). This time allows about a half-hour over standard for a steep descent from the Ridge.

Difficulties: Navigation easy and, except for the one steep descent, the terrain is good. However for the full route you face a lot of climbing and even the escape route is physically demanding.

Map: Sheet 78 or 1:25 000 "Macgillycuddy's Reeks".

Route: From the carpark take the well-worn path into the Hag's Glen, keeping to the route indicated by at least one arrow. This will mean fording two streams before reaching a track. From near the start the great pyramid of Carrauntoohil becomes increasingly prominent while, much nearer, you cannot mistake the great stump known as the Hag's Tooth (Teeth on the maps, though the other molars are not obvious - to me anyway).

Just before you come abreast of the Tooth the track crosses back over the main stream. Do not follow it. Instead keep to the north-west side of the valley to walk through a flat boulder field and pick up a rough path rising high above Lough Gouragh. It is obvious from here that the climb to the summit of Carrauntoohil is going to be tough, and equally obvious that the wild, dramatic and stern grandeur all around is going to be an ample reward for your efforts. The steep climb, all on path ends in a tiny flat area to the right of which towers a slender rock pinnacle. Keep the stream on the left to ascend to a similar flat area and climb onward, still following the stream to arrive at Cumeenoughter Lake (GR 8480), set magnificently with cliffs rising in most directions. A good place for a break.

There are two grassy gullies rising from the lake, to the north-west and the south; the latter is next to be climbed (if you want to traverse almost the entire Beenkeragh Ridge, climb the north-west gully). Take a path upwards, great bulges of cliff on both sides, to reach the Beenkeragh Ridge. Turn left (south-east) here and walk over rocky but easy ground to the summit of Carrauntoohil (1039m, 3.25 hours). Wasn't it worth the effort!

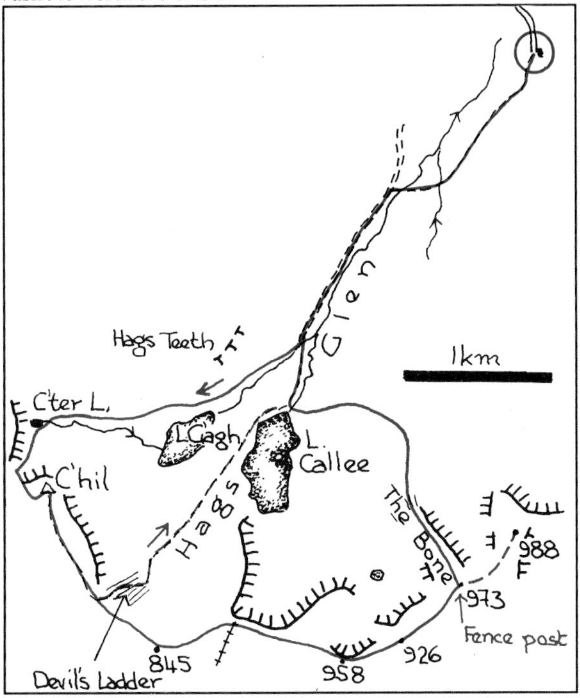

The descent south is easy and a bit of an anti-climax, down an eroded path bordered by unnecessary cairns. The col at the top of the Devil's Ladder is the start of the escape route, useful if the weather is bad. Take care on the slippery and eroded ground.

If you want to go on, the glory of the Reeks Ridge awaits, whose majesty I have to compress into a dull recital of names. Climb both summits of Cnoc na Toinne (845m and over 820m), crossing a fence on the descent from the second and then climb steeply to Cnoc an Chuillinn (958m). From here follow the crest of the Ridge to climb the undistinguished summit pt 926m and then push on to Maolán Bui (973m, 6 hours). Watch out for the rusty iron fence post here; it marks the point of descent along the Bone, a rocky spur reaching towards the Hag's Glen. Remember that some of the walk along the Bone is going to be slow. Still, if you have the energy it is worth while walking there and back to Cnoc na Péiste to view the jagged, narrow section of the Ridge. That done, return to the fence post and start down north-west along the Bone.

The Bone gives easy walking for a few hundred metres. Then its character suddenly changes, with a steep descent through boulders. Pretty tiring at the end of a long day, so take it easy. After no more than 200m distance along this tough descent - it seems longer - the spur starts to divide and it is easier to swing right with the grassier sub-spur even though this may mean retracing steps to cross the outlet stream from Lough Callee at the lough. (Alternatively, you can simply follow the stream down without crossing it until the track obligingly crosses over to meet you.)

Once across the outlet stream, pick up the track along the Hag's Glen and retrace steps all the way to the start.

ROUTE 22: REEKS RIDGE FROM BLACK VALLEY

A steep and direct approach from the area of Black Valley youth hostel (or possibly Glencar) to the spectacular Reeks Ridge, whose great cliffs overlook corrie lakes and beyond them the plains of Kerry. With much of the narrow, rocky arête over 900m, rising to 988m at Cnoc na Péiste, this is no place for the faint-hearted.

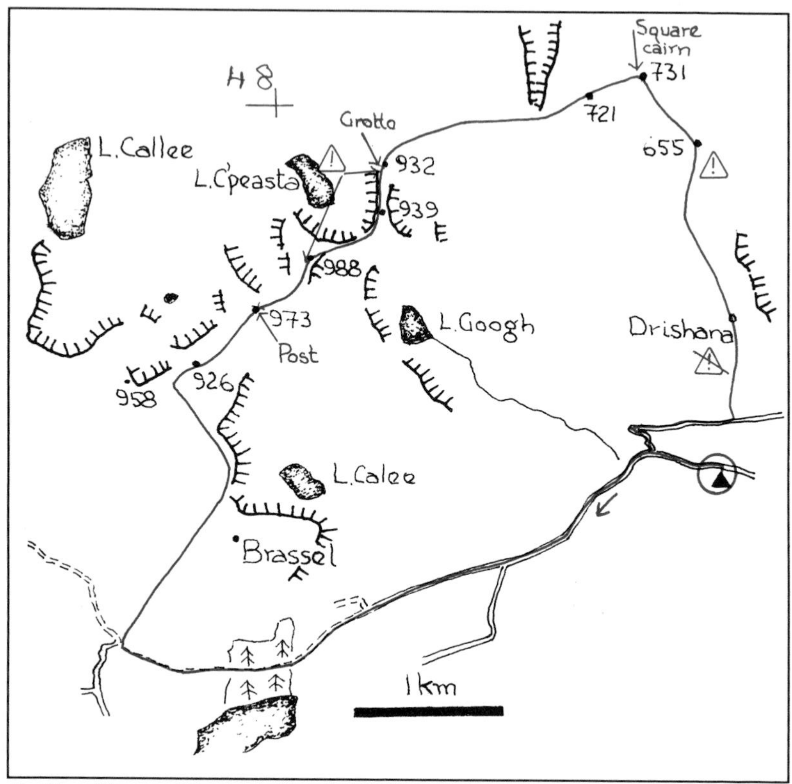

Getting There: The route is suitable if you are staying at Black Valley youth hostel (GR 8682), but if you are staying in the Glencar (GR 7284) area you can easily adapt it by starting in the same place as route 23.

Walking Time: About 7.5 hours (distance 17km, climb 1250m), allowing about 1 hour extra for slow going over exposed terrain on the Ridge. Surprisingly, there are several options to shorten the route.

Difficulties: Vertigo is the main problem. For a well-defined stretch of about 1km the ridge is narrow, rocky and steep-sided. Navigational problems are minor.

Map: 1:25 000 "Macgillycuddy's Reeks", which clearly shows the cliffs and steep ground on each side of the Ridge, is more useful than the alternative, sheet 78. Because of lack of space the sketch map given here identifies mountains on the Ridge only by their heights. No disrespect intended.

Route: Turn left out of the hostel to follow the Kerry Way westward on road for 3km or so. Still on it, enter forest on a normally very wet path, not helped by boulders underfoot and continue on a better path on the other side of the forest.

Where the Way goes straight ahead and a barely motorable road heads down to the left you must gird your loins for a steep climb.

The task now is to reach the Ridge, a direct and unrelenting climb of 800m generally north, which offers increasingly spectacular views in all directions. On the way you may like to climb to the top of Brassel Mountain, which involves only a small additional climb.

There is no mistaking the crest of the Ridge, which you should reach at about pt 926m (3.5 hours): your onward climb is halted by steeply plunging cliffs ahead. Turn right here and climb Maolán Buí (973m), whose summit has a solitary iron post, a useful landmark since there is no other for miles around. From here walk onwards to nearby Cnoc na Péiste (988m).

So far, so vertigo-free. The next section, the kilometre from here over the Big Gun (939m) and thence on the left-ward swing to Cruach Mhór (932m) involves some scrambling and requires care and time. Conventional wisdom suggests that you keep to the right on the first section as far as the Big Gun (939m) and to the left thereafter, but you will have to pick a route for yourself, using vestigial paths here and there. It may be some consolation to know that there is a prominent man-made block of stones on Cruach Mhór so that the end of the vertigo-full section is clearly visible from afar.

The block of stones on Cruach Mhór, which is about 3m high (the block, not the mountain), turns out to be a grotto and contains a tiny statue: a bit disproportionate. From the summit descend east along the rocky, narrow ridge, mercifully with the fear of vertigo now behind. After passing the narrow col to the south of Loch an Chaca, the ridge broadens and assumes a less threatening aspect and it is an easy climb to Cnoc an Bhráca (731m), which is crowned by a fine cairn of square cross-section. With the Purple Mountain Group now dominating the eastern skyline, turn south-west from the summit to climb nearby Cnoc an dTarbh, which has a heap of boulders on its summit, and continue south over rough country to Drisean (664m), which you may climb without realising it, so insignificant is the rise to the summit. Descend directly south from Drisean, climbing fences with care. Turn right when you reach the road - do not head across country - and walk the short distance to the hostel.

Escape Routes: Allowing for the fact that one person's easy escape route might be another's death fall, the "Macgillycuddy's Reeks" map (and the sketch map given here) indicates cliffs accurately. You can see from it that you can retreat cautiously from more than a few points. Though fairly prone to vertigo, I have retreated south from the Big Gun, where the contours seem to be alarmingly close together, without too much bother.

ROUTE 23: BROAGHNABINNIA AND STUMPA DULOIGH

An initial long and unrelenting climb (partly avoidable) is followed by spectacular terrain both near at hand and further away, where most of the Reeks, as well as whole ranges of other mountains are visible in all directions.

Getting There: A remote starting point in Bridia valley about 6 miles (10km) from Glencar, reached by a very poor road. From Junction B (see page 2) head towards Ballaghbeama Gap. After about 1½ miles continue straight ahead where the main road swings sharply right and drive about 4 miles (6km) to a gate at the end of the road, looking out just before that for places to park considerately (GR 788817). If driving from Ballaghbeama Gap watch out for the sign for Cloon Lough and turn right shortly thereafter at the tee.

Walking Time: 7 hours (distance 15km, climb 1300m), including 0.75 hours for one steep descent. The variation reduces the formidable total climb.

Difficulties: Some minor crags to negotiate initially. To find the correct point for the descent to Gearhameen River requires careful attention to navigation.

Map: Sheet 78 or 1:25 000 "Macgillycuddy's Reeks", the latter showing the contour lines much more clearly.

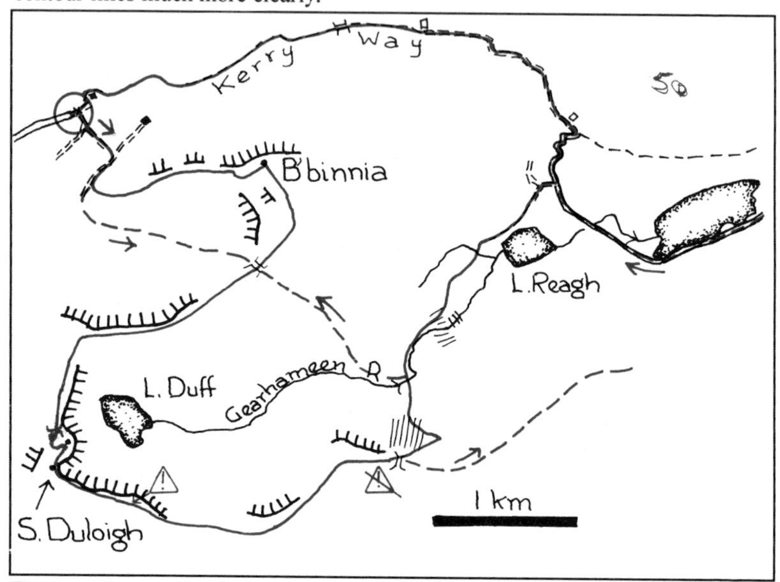

Route: The massive bulk of Broaghnabinnia dominates the view east and south from the start and it's all too obvious that a stiff climb lies ahead.

Cross the gate onto a track and turn right immediately onto another track. Fork shortly left and take this track to its end after a short distance. Continue straight ahead on rough ground to cross a nearby stream and ascend to a grassy track where you turn right. This track shows no upward inclination, so after a few minutes' walking you will have to turn left off it and ascend Broaghnabinnia using a ramp heading roughly east.

This ramp is bordered by steep ground; giving an easily recognisable route to the

summit with only one or two crags to be negotiated, all at the start. Near the summit the fence that runs along the ramp for most of the way takes a rightward lurch. Here you should closely follow it to avoid cliffs facing north-west.

The summit of Broaghnabinnia (745m, 2 hours), a tiny plain of boggy grass, is disappointing, but the views especially northwards where Carrauntoohil dominates, are magnificent. From the summit head towards the col to the south, veering left of the direct line if crags or steep ground threaten. From the col follow the rising spur running west in a series of rocky ledges, a spur offering splendid views into the corrie cradling Lough Duff. In fact, the varying views of Lough Duff and its corrie will continue for some time to come.

After about 45 minutes from the col the spur turns abruptly south, now with formidable cliffs on the left and steep ground to the right. A tiny but distinct col precedes the short but stiff climb to the northern summit of Stumpa Duloigh (776m); to avoid vertigo simply veer right of the direct line to tackle it and the slightly higher southern summit (784m).

From here the high ground turns abruptly again to the east, giving easy walking over grass. The ground falls gradually for about 1km and then descends sharply. It is from the end of this descent that you should pay careful attention to navigation, because from here on the terrain is not much help in finding the exact point from which to descend to Gearhameen River. So, keeping steep ground close on the left, walk a kilometre further over undulating ground, after which you will be confronted by a sustained rise. Descend left from here, veering right of the direct descent to avoid crags, and when below them veer sharply back again to reach Gearhameen River. (If you miss this descent point make sure you descend further on, where the ground is not so steep and not before, where it is steeper.)

The walk by Gearhameen River (keep it on the right) is lovely, but not without its hazards. Where it cascades as a waterfall, you must veer away from it to make your way between crags overlooking Lough Reagh. When below the crags take the path along the western shore of the lake, cross a gate, walk the few metres of track beyond to a tee, turn right, walk to the nearby road and turn left.

This road climbs sharply to reach the Kerry Way, at this point a track. Turn left here and follow it over a broad col separating Black Valley from Bridia Valley where you started. The waymarking is easy to follow as far as the descent into Bridia, where it seems to falter. If you lose it head for the nearby farmhouse on the right of the valley, the one which was close at hand at the start, and walk round its back. From here the start is only a short distance away.

Easier Variation. Broaghnabinnia is not the most enticing of mountains. You can reduce the climb by over 300m by climbing initially to the col to its south and picking up the route from here.

Black Valley Variation. From the hostel walk south of Cummeenduff Loughs to reach Lough Reagh, ascend to the col south of Broaghnabinnia, take the main route from here but instead of descending to Lough Reagh, continue east to descend to the road from the west of the corrie at GR 8480. Walking time is 7.25 hours (distance 21km, climb 980m), but the walking distance may be reduced by driving to GR 8481.

NORTH IVERAGH

North Iveragh consists of the area west of Lough Caragh and north of the road running from Cahersiveen through Ballaghisheen Gap (GR 6779). There is much easy walking, which degenerates into plain dull and bland in places. The most memorable part is undoubtedly the line of great corries of which Coomasaharn is the most notable (routes 24, 26). Other walking in the area is less spectacular, though remote Colly offers excellent, easy walking (route 28) and other parts give good long-distance views of coast or lake (routes 25, 27).

ROUTE 24: COOMASAHARN LAKESHORE

A short walk but not an easy one, with some difficult negotiating around lakeshore crags. In particular, the eastern shore of Coomasaharn Lake is tough but rewarding territory, encompassing spectacular close-at-hand views of waterfalls and towering cliffs. If you want to make life easy but unexciting, walk the western shore only.

Getting There: Start at the same point as route 26.

Walking Time: In theory this is a walk of 4km with practically no climbing and so should take an hour. You might do it in that time if you walk a there-and-back along the western shore. However you could easily spend 3 hours or more if you want to do the entire route and so explore the area fully.

Difficulties: Some crags that are quite difficult to negotiate after rain.

Map: Sheet 78 or 83 though hardly needed. The sketch map for this route is given with route 26.

Route: Take the track from the parking place to cross the nearby bridge and continue along it until it ends. From here take an intermittent path past a small peninsula. Soon after follow a distinct path by the lakeshore.

The difficult part now looms. At lakeshore level pass below the cascades of the stream pouring down from Coomacullen Lake and then keep about 10-15m above the shore, picking your way between crags and steep grassy slopes until you are across a second stream (or rather second cascade), that from Loughacummeen.

From here on it is easy to keep to the lakeshore. However rather than marching directly back, why not follow the third stream into its valley, climbing the several steps over which the stream plunges and admiring the mighty cliffs which abruptly terminate the eastern side of Termoyle Mountain.

That done, keep the lakeshore on the right to pass a dome-shaped rocky promontory and a small wooded island, before crossing rough fields to meet a gate. Take the grassy track beyond to the initial track of the day and walk the short distance to the start.

ROUTE 25: SEEFIN

Seefin (493m) itself is a mundane mound though it gives good views over Lough Caragh, its pleasantly wooded shore and the wide expanse of seashore about Rosbeigh. The return is by track along the Kerry Way. The upland section of the route forms an attractive alternative to the Way.

Getting There: Though four roads (and a track) converge at the start (at GR 703910), this is a none too accessible place. The easiest way is to drive 1.4

miles (2.2km) east of Glenbeigh on the N70 and here take the side road on the right bearing a Kerry Way marker. Drive for about a mile to the aforementioned cross roads. You can also reach this point from the road along the west side of Lough Caragh. **Buses:** Timetable 279 or 280 along the N70.

Walking Time: 3 hours (distance 10km, climb 320m), half of which is on track.

Difficulties: None.

Map: Sheet 78.

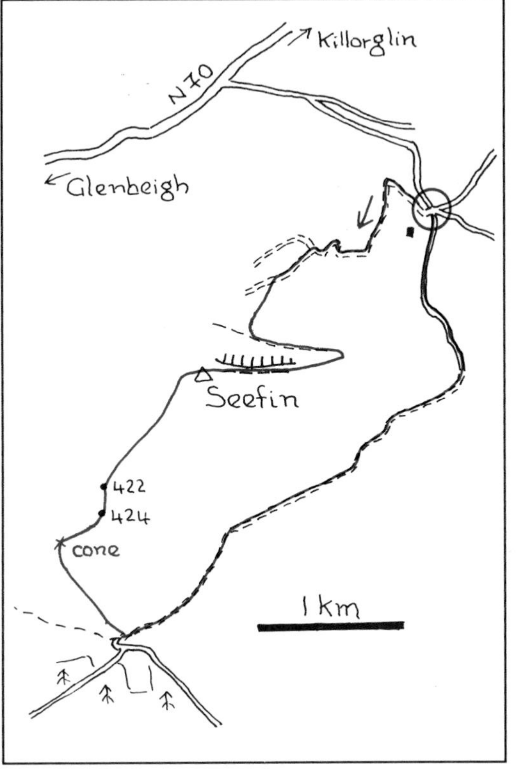

Route: Take the track at the cross roads, keeping with it until you reach a plateau on the northern side of Seefin, which is cut up by turf workings. At any convenient point leave it to head south for what looks like another good track heading gently upward across the north-facing side of Seefin.

Except it isn't a good track, as you will see when you reach it. Instead it is a narrow, rough path which is little easier to negotiate than the surrounding country. Where it finally peters out on the eastern spur of Seefin turn west and follow a fence and an intermittent path, the latter useful to avoid high heather. Climb to pt 443m and then walk along a clifftop overlooking a half-hearted corrie on the right.

Seefin (493m) has a trig pillar so you can't miss it, nor can you miss the prominent cairn 50m or so further on. From this viewpoint you can study much of the rest of the route: a long stretch of moorland off to the south-west, its monotony broken by a heap of boulders and beyond it, a curious cone rising above the general of the moorland (one or other of these is described as "Giant's Seat" on the half-inch map).

When you reach this cone a compass bearing of about 140° might be prudent as it is not obvious which way to go (it wasn't to me anyway). This bearing will take you down to the Kerry Way. Turn left here and walk over 4km back to the start through upland country offering good views over Lough Caragh and beyond.

ROUTE 26: GLENBEIGH CORRIES

A steep initial climb ends in a gentle walk with moorland on one side and a line of magnificent corries on the other, that holding Coomasaharn Lake being particularly impressive. The peaks themselves, of which Coomacarrea (772m) is the highest, are undistinguished. Two possible descents, one by a narrow but safe path along an arête between two of the corries, are given below.

Getting There: From Killarney (distance 26 miles (42km)) take the N72 through Killorglin and, noting signs carefully in the town, take the N70 to Glenbeigh. In Glenbeigh fork left at the Towers Hotel and continue for 4.4 miles (7.1km) to a sharp bend to the right (GR 636852). There is parking for a few cars at a deserted house on the right just before this bend.

The start may also be reached from Cahirsiveen (16 miles (26km) by branching off the N70 at the second turn right after the N70 passes under a bridge (at GR 6289). You will need a map to find the start from this direction. **Buses:** Timetable 279 or 280. If travelling by bus you can modify the walk to start and/or end at Mountain Stage (GR 6289) or the junction just to its east.

Walking Time: 6 hours (distance 16km, climb 940m) including a little time for the steep descent.

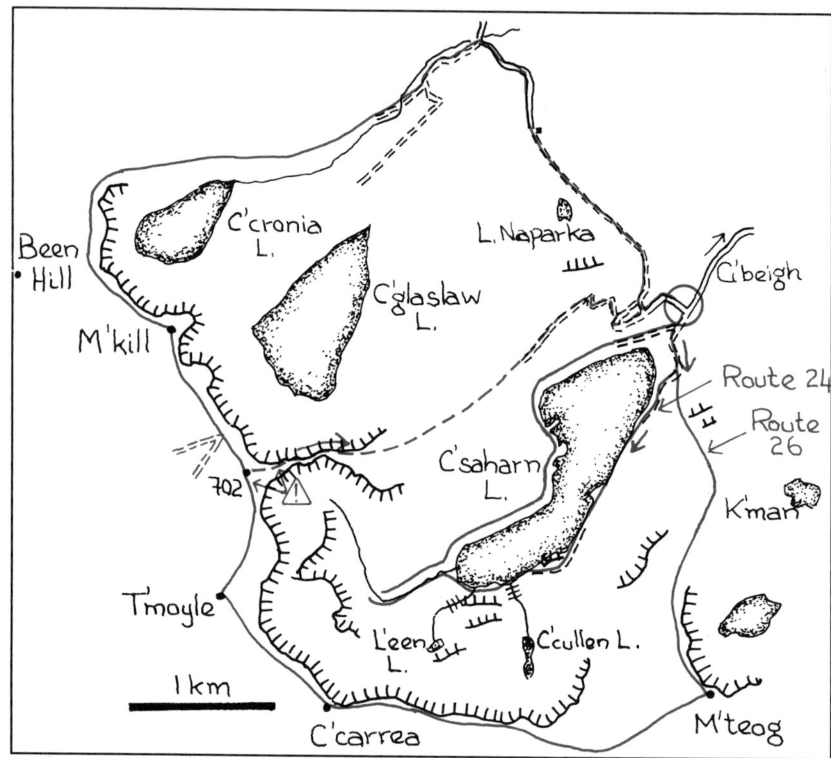

Difficulties: With unmistakable cliffs almost everywhere close at hand, navigation is easy, though if you are on the short variation (see below) in bad visibility take care that you find the correct point at which to descend towards Coomreagh (as described below). Underfoot conditions, though boggy for much of the route are not so bad as to cause delays.

Map: Sheet 78 or 83.

Route: From the bend, take the track across a nearby bridge and choose any convenient place beyond it to turn left off the track and climb steeply through rocky outcrops to Knocknaman (561m), a shoulder rather than a summit.

Now on comparatively gently rising ground head south, keeping initially to the crest of the spur. Then gradually veer left off it to climb Meenteog (715m) from where you can study the fine corrie to its north. (In bad conditions don't risk this detour to Meenteog; simply keep steep ground on the right after Knocknaman.)

Walk west from Meenteog to the cliffs overlooking Coomasaharn Lake. Once at these cliffs you can relax. Navigation is simple - keep the cliffs on the right - and the views magnificent. Apart from a whole range of mountains, the huge corrie around Coomasaharn Lake is at your feet, a corrie with at least two other lakes sheltering in ledges among the cliffs. Later on, take a look at the jagged cliff edge, Leam a Soggarth, running at right angles to the main line of the cliffs.

But we are ahead of ourselves. From the low point to the west of Meenteog, climb sharply to Coomacarrea (772m), the highest point of the day, from where the cliffs swing gradually right. Teermoyle (760m, 3.25 hours) is reached after a gentle drop from Coomacarrea followed by a slight rise. Though an indistinct summit Teermoyle is important if you want to do the short variation (see below).

If you don't, continue with the cliffs on the right, passing a vee of track on the left and a good indication of your position, especially if you intended only the short variation! Pass the corrie holding Coomaglaslaw Lake, a pale imitation of the corrie passed earlier, and climb Mullaghnarkill (665m), crowned by large slabs of rock. *Note you cannot reach lower ground directly north-east from Mullaghnarkill.*

Instead you must contour round the eastern side of Been Hill (there is no need to climb it) before considering the descent on the north-western side of Coomnacronia Lake. This is not difficult: simply keep walking north until the line of the cliffs eases and you can veer right to make your way through rough ground to the outlet stream from the lake.

The rest is an easy 5km, mostly on track or path through upland bog and fields. Start by keeping the stream on the right until you meet a track, follow it across the stream (alas, no bridge) and continue down to tarmac, turning right here away from a bridge and a house. Walk to the end of the road and along its continuation as a track, closing gates carefully as you advance.

After you pass Lough Naparka the track rises sharply and bends to the right to reach a fork at a deserted house (the map confusingly shows this section of track as a road). Turn left here, left again onto the nearby road and left yet again to reach the nearby start.

Short Variation. From Teermoyle descend north to a large expanse of pebbles and soft ground around pt 702m. Here turn east to descend a grassy slope and so reach a narrow arête with a path winding along its top, beyond which is a rough triangle of grassy ground. From this ground descend roughly north-east to the road system near the start. Walking time is 4.25 hours (distance 11km, climb 750m).

ROUTE 27: KNOCKNADOBAR

Knocknadobar (691m) is a great formless mass of mountain, formless that is except for a few scenic corries on its northern side. In addition, it gives good seaward views northwards to the Dingle peninsula and east to the bulk of the mountains of Iveragh.

Getting There: From Cahersiveen (about 8 miles (13km) away) take the N70 towards Glenbeigh, turning left (signed) to park at the carpark overlooking the beach at Kells (GR 558879). The start is also within easy reach of Glenbeigh.

Buses: Timetables 279 or 280.

Walking Time: 5.5 hours (distance 15km, climb 840m), though this may be considerably shortened by omitting the climb to Knocknadobar or by parking your car somewhere on the road west of Kells (or both).

Difficulties: None.

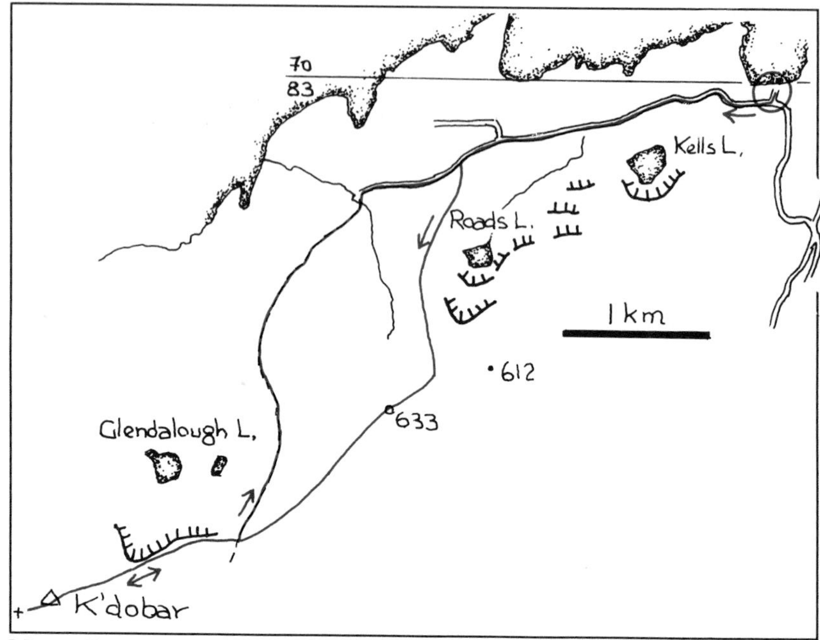

Map: Sheet 83. However, with much of the route right on the edge of this sheet, half-inch to the mile sheet 20 might be better as it gives an overall view of your surroundings.

Route: From the carpark turn right (west) and walk the narrow road towards the village of Roads. After about 2km continue straight ahead at a junction on the right bearing a waymark, but only for a few hundred metres. Here, with a bit of luck (required because there seems to be the prospect of further houses along this road) you will find unrestricted access to open country on the left.

Climb steadily upward, veering slightly left of a direct assault to aim for an impressive viewpoint close to the western side of Roads Lough, which is set in a deep corrie with fearsome cliffs to its south and rocky crags to its east. Continue upward past the corrie to reach a boggy col between pts 612m and 633m.

From here for some considerable time the underfoot conditions are firm, the slope is gentle and the views, which encompass a large part of Iveragh as well as the neighbouring Dingle peninsula are good. Climb pt 633m, then descend to the col on the eastern side of Knocknadobar. At the waymark at the far (western) end of this col you will have to decide whether to climb Knocknadobar (a stiff 200m climb which will take about an hour) or to take the easy variation (if so, skip to the paragraph after next), which means returning from here.

This there-and-back climb offers good views down onto the two lakes Glendalough over cliffs on the right and enhanced views in all directions. From the summit you may like to stroll a bit further to the large, solid cross. Strangely, this carries a lightning conductor, thus indicating some lack of confidence in God's undiluted approval of this structure.

Return to the col and the waymark and set off fairly steeply downhill and initially north on a rough waymarked path. The path eventually swings right to run parallel to an impressive coastline of cliff and what looks like an offshore island, though sheet 70 assures us that it is not. The path eventually drops to the scattered hamlet of Roads from where you have about 3km of pleasant walking back to the start at Kells.

Near Deelick Point (Route 2)

ROUTE 28: COLLY

A remote area close to the centre of the peninsula offers easy walking and navigation with good medium and long distance views but nothing exciting (and almost nothing dangerous) close at hand.

Getting There: The start (at GR 649783) is just west of Ballaghisheen Gap (GR 6779) at a junction on the north of the road. You will recognise it because it is the first junction west of the Gap that is out of forest. The start is within easy reach of Cahersiveen and Glencar.

Walking Time: 3.5 hours (distance 9km, climb 700m) including 3km on road.

Difficulties: With easy underfoot conditions and a clear route there should be few serious problems.

Map: Sheet 78 is better than sheet 83 in finding the start of the route but both are satisfactory.

Route: Walk up the track to reach a band of straggly forest on the left. A little way past its edge and within sight of the first (and only) house ahead, turn left off the track to walk uphill and follow the forest edge, which has at last developed a disciplined straight edge. (Incidentally the track shown on the 1:50 000 sheets wandering aimlessly for miles across the country around here seems to be, in part at least, a wall or earthbank.)

Walk to the upper end of the forest and continue directly upward beyond it, passing on the way an imposing rectangle of wall, or at least it would be a rectangle had it a fourth side. Pondering the intention of the builder of this strange edifice will lessen the pain of the ascent to the summit of Collybeg (over 530m), from where a large panorama opens up in all directions.

Collybeg is really the south-west spur of Colly, which is reached by a short but steep climb over easy ground. Colly (679m) commands excellent views with the edges of the great corries overlooking Coomasaharn Lake and its sister lakes prominent to the north-west and the sharp cone of Mullaghanattin off to the south-east.

A narrow ridge giving lovely views on both sides leads to Colly East (604m). From here descend south-east, thus heading for a rocky spur overlooking Ballaghisheen Gap. This spur offers somewhat tougher territory, with occasional outcrops and boggy areas to be negotiated, as well as a few rocky but minor peaks.

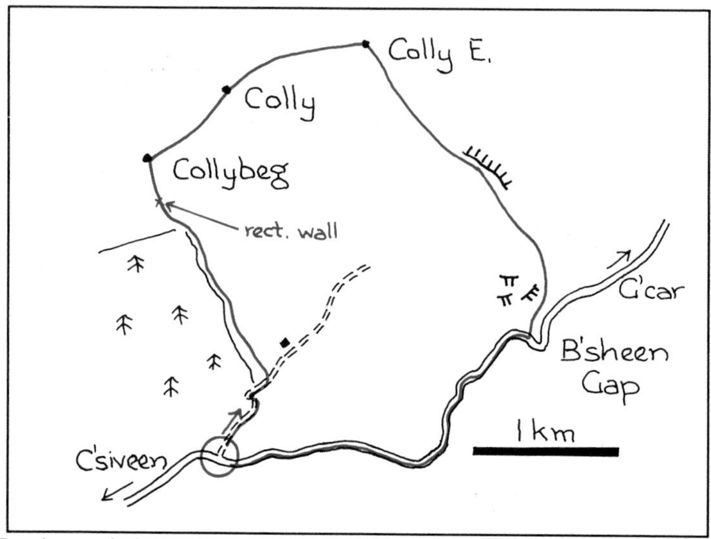

Tougher again is the descent to Ballaghisheen Gap over Knocknagapple (466m). This is the one area where you could come to grief, with small rocky outcrops to be carefully negotiated and with low but not insignificant cliffs on the left. If you want to make life easier for yourself keep close to the fence which runs just to the left of the crest of the spur. When you reach the Gap, turn right (of course) to walk 3km back to the start. It's mostly through forestry plantations but mercifully nearly all downhill so, though not over interesting, it shouldn't take too long.

SOUTH IVERAGH

South Iveragh consists of the mountains south of the road running from Cahersiveen through Ballaghisheen Gap and west of the road running through Ballaghbeama Gap. This is a great tangle of remote mountain, offering excellent walking ranging from easy going over short grass (routes 30, 31) to tough walking over extremely rocky terrain, sometimes with an abrupt transition from one to the other (routes 29, 33-35). Mullaghanattin (773m) (route 32) is the highest peak in the area and its characteristic Matterhorn-shaped summit makes it recognisable from afar. Bolus Head (route 36) is one of several easy coastal walks in the area.

ROUTE 29: COOMAVOHER

A walk whose initial dullness soon dissipates as you advance into a long, narrow corrie that ends at a remote lake almost surrounded by high, rocky cliffs.

Getting There: The start is at a bridge (GR 632739) about 15 miles (24km) east of Cahersiveen and about 13 miles (21km) west of Glencar. One way of getting there is to cross south over the bridge at Junction A (see page 2). Set the milometer here, turn second left after 0.8 miles, turn left again at 3.2 miles and park at the bridge at 5.4 miles.

Walking Time: Because of difficult terrain give yourself at least 2 hours if you decide to do the walk as suggested (distance 6km, with about 100m of climbing.)

Difficulties: On the south side of the corrie take care in negotiating rocky detours above the lakeshore; allow plenty of time for slow going.

Map: Sheet 78 or 83, the latter useful in finding the start.

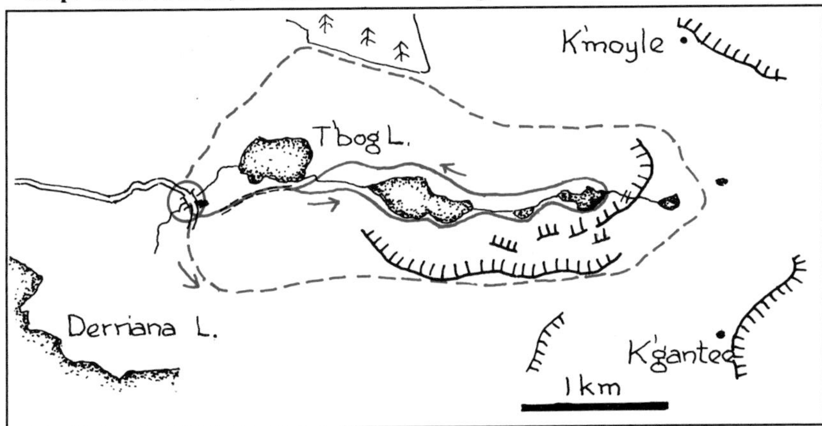

Route: The route as described follows the south side of the corrie on the outward journey and mostly the north side on the return. There is bog to the north of the first lake, Tooreenbog Lough, and slow going over steep ground on the south side of the corrie east of this lake, so you can walk south of Tooreenbog Lough and north of the other lakes on both the outward and return legs. Walkers are not noted for making life easy for themselves, and the route as described is more interesting. However you might like to take the easier route in adverse conditions.

Walk across the bridge (if you haven't already driven across it) and after the nearby first house on the left cross the first gate on this side and head eastward. Around here you should pick up a stretch of track which ends at Tooreenbog Lough and which is much preferable to the alternative slog across bogland.

From here on there is treacherous pathless terrain with some short but strenuous climbs to avoid rocky outcrops near the lakes, but no navigational difficulties.

At length you will come to the fourth and second last lake of the series - there is no mistaking it. A small lake hemmed in and almost surrounded by high, steep ground, some sections of which have more than a touch of cliff about them, this is a spectacular place. As for the fifth and last lake, you will see only the slender thread of waterfall which issues from it plunging down the cliffs at the head of the corrie.

As suggested above, you can return on the easier north side of the valley but to avoid the bog north of Tooreenbog Lough, cross the stream before you reach this lake and retrace steps from here on the southern side.

Higher Variation. I am indebted to Mortimer Moriarty of Cahersiveen for this suggestion, which gives easy underfoot conditions. From the above starting point, climb south to the spur along the south side of Coomavoher, turn east and walk round high ground almost surrounding the entire corrie. This walk can easily be extended to Knocknagantee or Knockmoyle. Walking time 3.25 hours (distance 9km, climb 520m).

ROUTE 30: EAGLES HILL

Not the most exciting country in Kerry, though allowing easy striding over gentle slopes overlooking the expanse of Lough Currane and the varied coastal area at the southern tip of the peninsula.

Getting There: Start in the village of Caherdaniel (GR 5559). Park considerately.

Walking Time: 5 hours (distance 15km, climb 700m).

Difficulties: Easy underfoot conditions. Navigation not too easy after Eagles Hill but in an area with no natural hazards this should not pose great dangers.

Map: Sheet 83 or 84.

Route: From the centre of the village take the Kerry Way uphill (east) on a narrow path which traverses a rough and rocky spur before dropping to 'Camomile Corner', so called because of the abundance of the plant which grows there. This is a junction of the Kerry Way and your route is the left, uphill branch.

This branch - it has now graduated to a track - heads steadily upward to Windy Gap, revealing a gradually widening panorama of lowland and coast down to the right. At the Gap (2.25 hours), a decision. It is marginally worth the effort (it will take about a half-hour in total) to climb to pt 459m just to the east to get a better view of the valley to the north. Though you will see all this from a different angle later, what you won't get another chance to see is Staigue Fort (1).

From the Gap, ascend steeply west to Eagles Hill (549m), avoiding a line of slabs parallel along your route. The summit does not quite live up to its impressive name, as it is only a grassy gently-sloped dome. As you will shortly see, much more grassy, gently sloping terrain lies ahead. From the summit walk south-west for about 1km to keep to the high ground, then swing north-west to pt 473m, which you are unlikely to recognise. What you should recognise however, is the end of a track a little further on. It's difficult to miss since it is so close to steep ground on the right, ground that you are unlikely to be traversing.

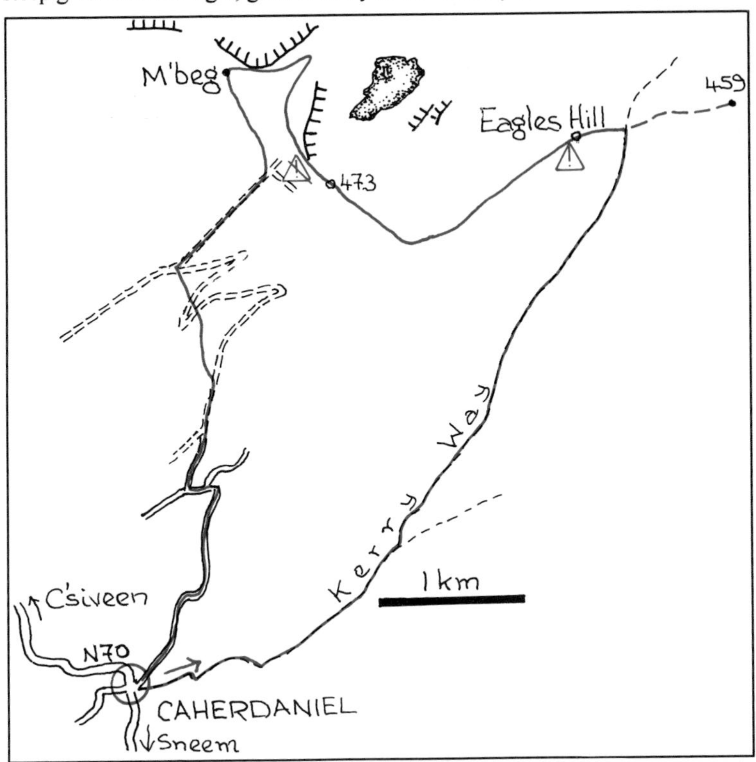

From this track it's worthwhile to detour north to the top of the spur running north-east from Mullaghbeg. This is a lovely eyrie, commanding views down into Coomrooanig Lough and north-west over expansive Lough Currane. From here climb the little way to the summit of Mullaghbeg (509m), from where you will readily observe that underfoot conditions to west and south-west are no more exciting than those you are now on.

The return to Caherdaniel is easy. Walk roughly south from Mullaghbeg to a bog track and turn right to reach a nearby junction. The junction running east descends towards Caherdaniel but if you prefer, you can descend steeply south ignoring the track until you reach it again at about the 150m contour line (no, it's not marked on the ground). Back on the track, walk downhill until it shortly improves to tarmac, take the fork left downhill at this point, fork left again shortly after and continue downhill through farming country back to Caherdaniel.

Note

(1) Staigue Fort dates from early in the Christian Era and is one of the finest in Ireland. It may have been used for defence. The walls are up to 4m high and 6m thick and the whole fort has a diameter of nearly 30m.

ROUTE 31: COOMCALLEE

To start and finish, a lot of track and road walking in varied, pleasant terrain. Between these, a walk along the high, 5km-long Coomcallee ridge, with some soft ground underfoot but overlooking some delectable territory.

Getting There: From Waterville (GR 5066) head south on the N70, shortly cross the bridge over the Currane River (and so signed) and take the next turn left. Drive onward for about 4 miles (7km) to a signpost for the Kerry Way. Turn left here and park on the left on waste ground a few hundred metres further on (GR 566652). As you can see from the sketch map you can also park anywhere suitable along the long road or track part of the route. **Buses:** Timetable 279, 280 buses to Waterville (and thereafter lucky lifts!).

Walking Time: 6 hours (distance 19km, climb 780m).

Difficulties: Quite easy, navigationally and underfoot, to the trig pillar on Coomcallee. Then more difficult navigation though still easy underfoot.

Map: Sheet 83 or 84.

Route: Take the Kerry Way north, island-dotted Lough Currane on the left. Alas, you won't see it for long, as the track unobligingly enters a thick wood.

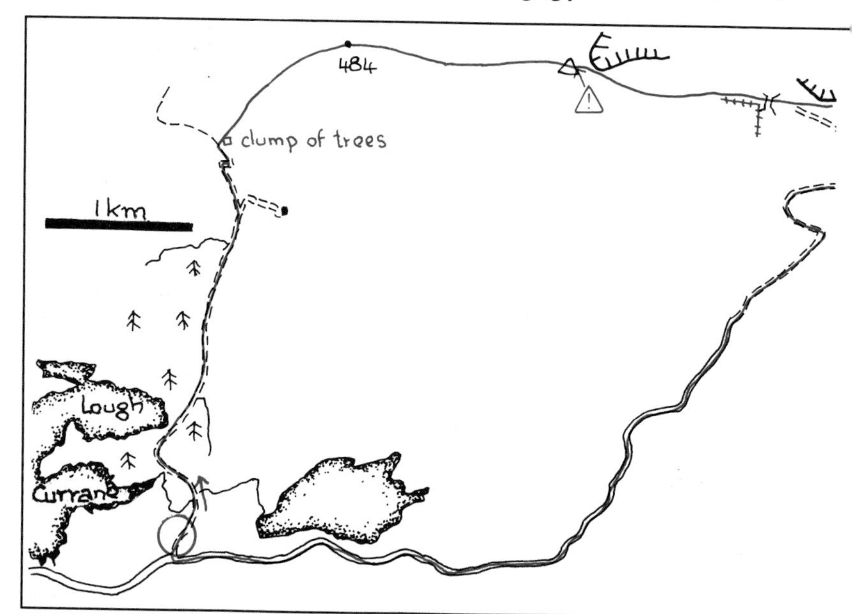

When the track - and you - finally re-emerge, with the lake not now evident, continue steadily uphill still on the Way, to close to the house perched near the crest of the spur ahead.

Walk to a small, dense clump of trees surrounded by thick stone walls a few hundred metres uphill of the house and continue upwards to pt 484m, avoiding gorse as best you can. Point 484m marks the start of the really good panorama: it is especially impressive to the north all the way to the far end of the long Coomcallee ridge.

Climb steeply on a narrow, rocky ridge to the western end of the Coomcallee ridge and continue to the trig pillar at pt 675m (2.75 hours) set in a plateau of short grass which extends with undulations for another 3km eastwards.

After pt 675m a little care is required in navigation. In bad conditions it might be prudent to walk directly on a bearing from the trig pillar to the col in GR 6068. Otherwise, walk to the bouldery corrie just to the east of pt 675m and from there descend gently east towards the col in GR 6068, on the near side of which is a set of old fence posts, which may be a navigational reassurance. From here it is worth the extra effort to look down over the next two corries to the north of the plateau before tackling Coomcallee (650m) (don't worry about the indistinct 642m). The summit is an unimpressive mound of grass and peat hags crisscrossed by sturdy fences, but the views are impressive and wide-ranging.

From the summit retrace steps towards the col, veering south from it as you approach to pick up an old track. Once on it, keep to it! It will take you down to the end of the road, from where it is 5km on country roads, through varied, scenic and remote surroundings back to the start.

Adventurous Variation. My wife and myself innocently thought it would be easy enough to walk south from Coomcallee (650m) and take in the whole ridge to Windy Gap (GR 5863), where we could pick up the Kerry Way. The first kilometre or so was easy. After that it took an hour to struggle over crags, around boulders and across cols to Lough Sallagh, from where we retreated, bloody and bowed. It looks as though the terrain improves as you continue on the ridge, so if you have plenty of time or more agility than we (in the last flush of middle age) you might try it. Note that the forest does not extend to the crest of the ridge as shown on the 1:50 000 maps.

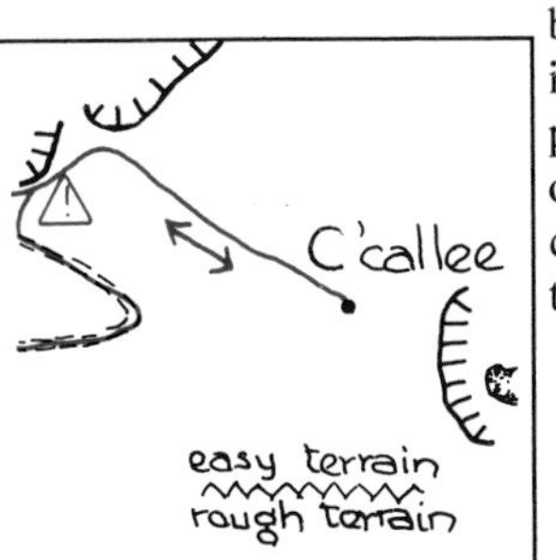

ROUTE 32: MULLAGHANATTIN FROM THE SOUTH

A splendid high-level walk, much of it along a narrow ridge with superb views in all directions, culminating in the sharp peak of Mullaghanattin (773m). Only the broader eastern end is a trifle dull underfoot but the views continue to be superb.

Getting There: A long and slow drive from any direction. From Killarney (23 miles (37km)) take the N71 and R568 (at Moll's Gap), turn right at the second of two close-together turns after about 6 miles (10km) from Moll's Gap (signed Ballaghbeama Gap), continue straight ahead after 1.4 miles (2.3km), where the main road swings right. Park (at GR 746746) at the turn left after another 1.9 miles (3.1km).

From Glencar (12 miles (19km)) take the road initially west to Junction B (see page 2), turn left here to cross Ballaghbeama Gap. Turn left about 3½ miles (6km) beyond the Gap. Park at the turn left after another 1.9 miles (3.1km).

Bus: Timetable 280, which travels along the R568.

Walking Time: 4.5 hours (distance 10km, climb 1000m).

Difficulties: A usually wet descent at the end, otherwise fairly good underfoot. Navigation is generally easy but in this remote area care is always essential.

Note that there is a fence (or in a few places boundary stones) from north-west of the first summit pt 531m, all the way along the route to the col east of Mullaghanattin, except that veers south of this summit.

Map: Sheet 78. Most the route is also covered on the 1:25 000 map.

Route: Don't panic! The distinctive Matterhorn-like peak of Mullaghanattin is nowhere to be seen as you emerge from your car, but you are not (necessarily) at the wrong starting place. Perversely the summit can be seen clearly from almost anywhere except the start.

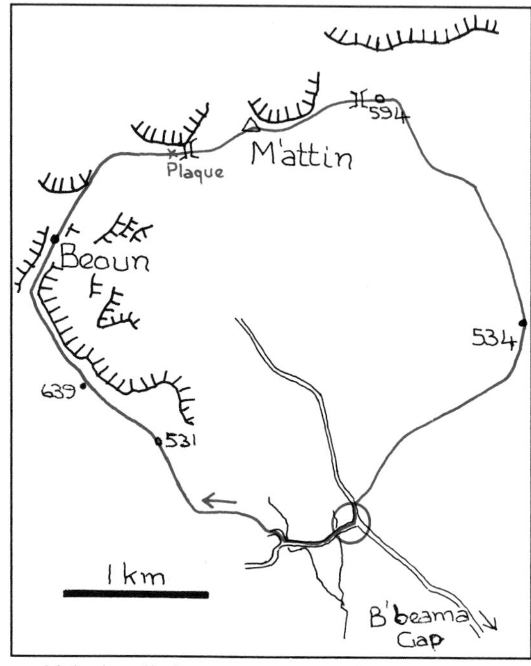

I have chosen a clock-wise circuit because it is easier to cut the route short from the eastern side at the end of the day rather than via the cliffy descent of the west. There may be factors which might dictate that you walk anti-clockwise. Either way the route directions will be equally intelligible.

Take the turn left (west) to the nearby first farm and ask permission here to go through the yard. The slabby rocks of the first peak lie directly behind the farm and it is straight climb to the nearly level area around pt 531m, after which the climb resumes to pt 639m. The route from here on is pure joy: a narrow ridge, marvellous views and no navigational problems. After Beoun (752m) the route swings east over some rocky hummocks to face Mullaghanattin itself. Before the summit a small plaque commemorating a climber who died in an accident here may be some reassurance that you are on course (given its nature, maybe it won't be too reassuring in other respects).

The long climb to the summit ends at the trig pillar of Mullaghanattin (3.25 hours) and predictably marvellous views. One navigational point to note is that you must swing right at point 594m and so face a boggy broad spur running south. The only feature of note on this spur is the unexpected band of slabby rock across the route before pt 534m, in bad visibility an indication that you must swing south-west at the next summit to reach the start. The descent is boggy and steep, a slight anti-climax, but unlikely to impair what should have been an enjoyable day.

ROUTE 33: FINNARARAGH FROM CLOON LOUGH

A lovely, memorable walk in stern and exciting terrain. A wealth of varied underfoot conditions ranging from bogland to rocky domes and with dramatic (or maybe terrifying!) views near at hand and further away. In a remote area with difficult navigation and terrain this is not a place for the novice or inexperienced.

Getting There: From Killarney the total distance is about 25 miles (40km) and the time not much less than 1 hour. Drive to Glencar, continue straight ahead to Junction B (see page 2), turn left here towards Ballaghbeama Gap, turn right to keep on the main road, take the next turn right (signed) to Cloon Lough. Park about 2 miles (3km) further on at waste ground near the bridge at the lake (GR 709789). This point may also be reached from south Iveragh by crossing Ballaghbeama Gap, a very slow road.

Walking Time: 8 hours (distance 18km, climb 1180m). This allows a generous (or is it?) 1.25 hours over standard for difficult navigation and a steep descent. There are some limited opportunities to cut the walk short.

Difficulties: As indicated in the first paragraph this is not a route for the faint-hearted (or indeed even for the stout-hearted in bad conditions). Navigation is quite difficult in mountains with few good landmarks, where you could easily wander off the route in bad weather into quite unforgiving terrain.

Map: Sheet 78. Some of the route is on the 25 000 "MacGillycuddy's Reeks" map.

Coomalougha Cliffs (Route 33)

Route: Take the track on the right of the lake, at the fork go left to pass a deserted building. The track continues for a while after this but you should leave it about here to climb through rough ground, aiming for a tiny col to the west (specifically at GR 681768).

At the col the next task is clear: to climb to pt 666m to the south. The terrain, quite evident well before reaching the col, is also clear: mighty layers of bare rock contorted into a spur of tight folds and whorls. Splendid but difficult terrain. Luckily, there is a grassy ramp just to the left of the crest of the spur which gives much easier walking.

Thus facilitated, you should arrive without too much loss of energy on the plateau just north of pt 666m, on which plateau rocky outcrops yield abruptly to gentle moorland. Climb pt 666m, an indistinct summit in moorland and continue roughly south over boggy land to pt 636m, passing on the way great slabs of rock around Coomalougha Lough on the left and the rocky defile east of Knocknagantee on the right, both examples of the sudden changes in terrain in this area. (By the way, if you want an escape route here, look at the end of route 35.)

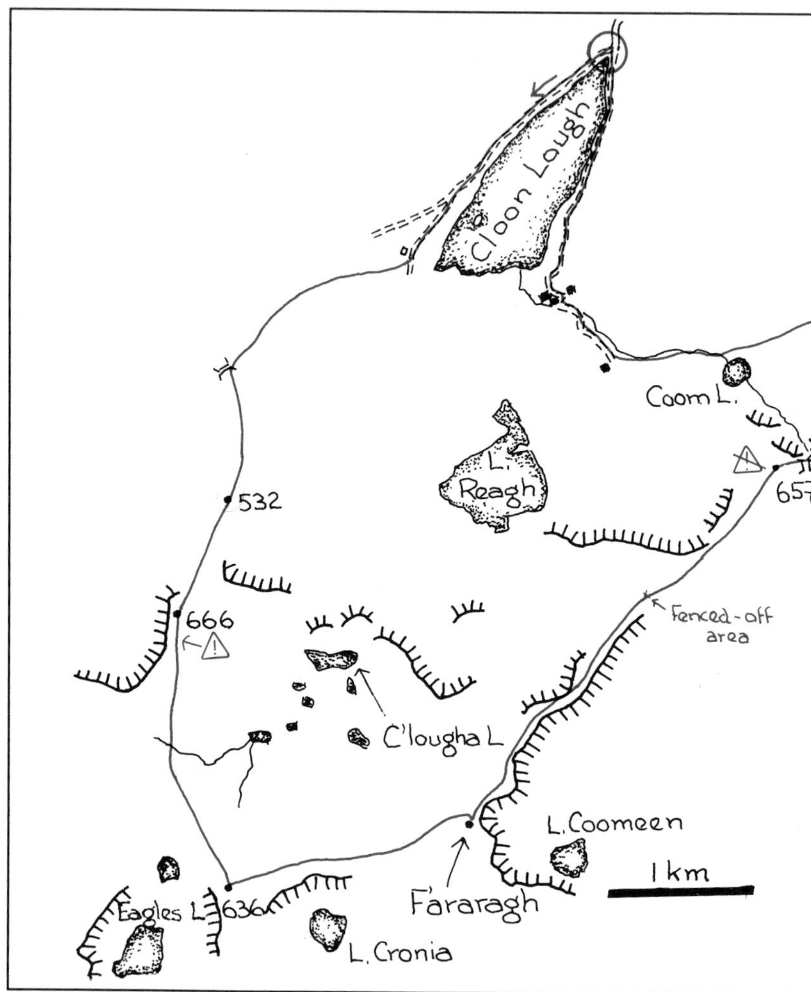

From pt 636m the next target is Finnararagh to the east. This is easy terrain; a slight dip north of Lough Coomnacronia is followed by a general rise on which there are two small lakes, meagre enough landmarks. Along here rocky outcrops start to appear, some looking like irregular stacks of stone books. The summit of Finnararagh (667m, 3.75 hours) is slightly off the direct line of the route; its small cairn on a grassy mound overlooks an expanse of mountain valley and lowland to the south and a rocky undulating ridge stretching away to the north-east.

This is the difficult ridge to be tackled next, difficult but magnificent. You can climb all the domes of bare rock along it if you wish, but for the average soul it is difficult enough even to negotiate round them. The important thing is to keep to the ridge; it falls away steeply in convoluted strata on the right but comparatively gently on the left, so take care not to wander off in that direction.

Over 1km from Finnararagh the ridge drops slightly and swings north for a few hundred metres before resuming its march north-east. At about here the severity of the terrain eases somewhat, with grassy areas and rocky outcrops, one or two contorted into perfect arcs sheltering a variety of plants. Here again it is difficult to pinpoint the high points on this ridge; a tiny fenced-off area is marked on the sketch map, and this may be some reassurance that you are on the right route.

What is really unmistakable however is the steep drop into a narrow grassy col to the south-east of Coom Lough. From here it is an equally steep climb to Beoun (752m, 6.5 hours), a long grassy ridge falling in cliffs on the right and in crags and steep ground on the left.

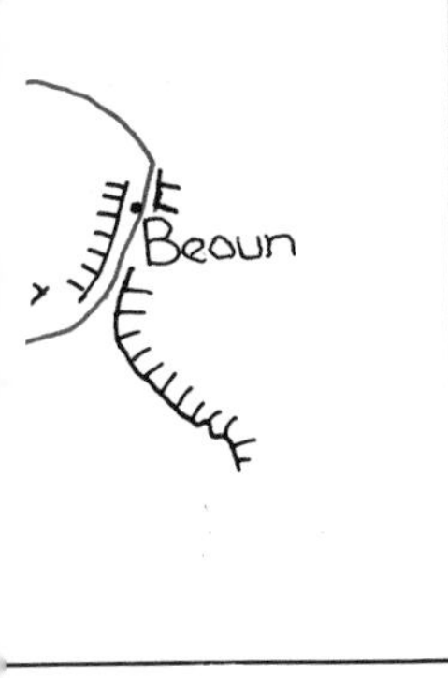

Drop north-east from the summit for a short distance and then swing north-west onto rocky ground, heading for Coom Lough. This is a tough descent at the end of a long day so take care. When you reach the lough cross over the outlet stream and follow it to the nearest house, where a track begins. This will take you down through a cluster of houses (the network of roads shown on sheet 78 do not appear to exist) and onto a track running along the shore of Cloon Lough. And here, for once on this route, you can't go wrong!

Variations. Route 35 gives another, contrasting way of starting this route. Basically you are trading the early climb to a high level (and panoramic views) as described above, for a low-level bog-trot and the close-up splendours of the mighty cliffs south-west of Lough Reagh, followed by a steep climb.

It looks possible to shorten the route by walking north-west from the ridge south-west of pt 657m, though I haven't tried it myself. What I have done is to climb down from the col to the south-east of Coom Lough. This involves some undignified scrambling down ledges, without knowing if the next ledge is going to be possible to negotiate. It is not an experience I would wish to repeat.

ROUTE 34: KNOCKNAGANTEE

Sudden changes in terrain characterize this route: gently sloped bogland gives way to rocky boulders and a great bulge of protruding cliff about Eagles Lough; high moorland west of Knocknagantee yields abruptly to a difficult terrain of rocky slabs and hidden lakes. A route that can easily be varied and specifically the more difficult section omitted.

Getting There: This requires some attention. Cross west over the bridge in the centre of Sneem (the east side has the post office), fork right at the triangle, and turn right at its end (here set your milometer). Pass the sports ground at 0.2 miles, fork next left, pass a narrow road heading sharply back on the left and at 3.0 miles turn left at a tee. Drive onward to 3.5 miles to park on waste ground before a bridge (GR 669712). **Buses:** Timetable 270 or 280 buses to Sneem could be useful, leaving at least an hour's walk at each end (courage, you might get a lift).

Walking Time: 5.5 hours (distance 13km, climb 1000m), thus allowing an extra half-hour for rough terrain (this section can be avoided).
Difficulties: Details of the rough terrain are given below and its location shown on the sketch map. Otherwise good underfoot conditions and fairly easy navigation.

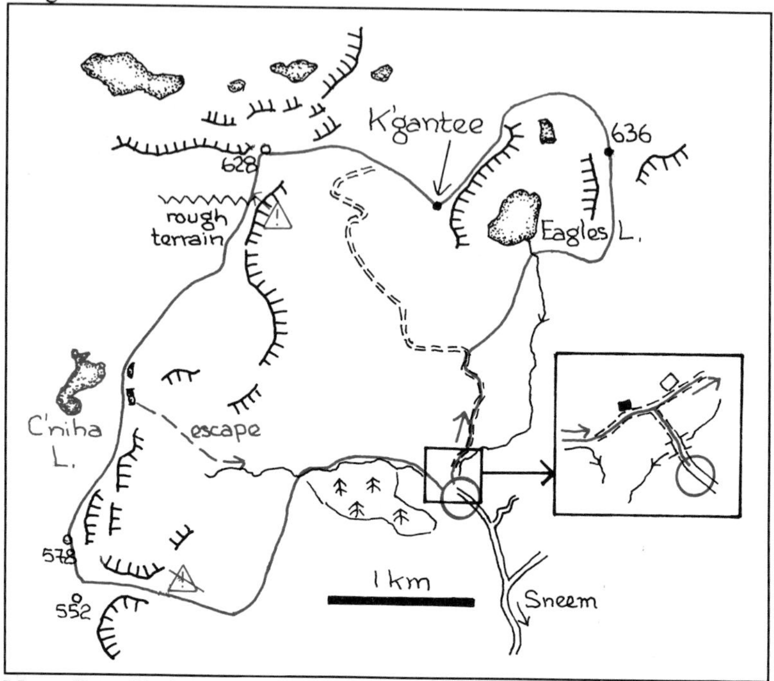

Map: Sheet 83 shows most of the approach road and the route except for a tiny section to the east, while sheet 78 (preferable) shows the whole route but not the southern end of the approach road.
Route: Cross the bridge before the farm buildings, turn right at the tee and continue upwards heading roughly north on sloping moorland. After 20 minutes or more the track veers off to the left and levels off. This is about the point where you should leave it and head north-east across rough ground to the outlet stream from Eagles Lough. As you advance the great bulging cliffs on your left overlooking the lake become more impressive and dominant, but it is only when you reach the outlet stream near the lake and view the rugged corrie that its full splendour becomes apparent.

What I hope also won't become apparent is that you cannot cross the outlet stream. If this is so there is nothing for it but to walk round the lake, or indeed halfway round where you will be rightly tempted to climb the steep ground to the north of the lake, thus making a major diversion.

Anyway, let's assume you can cross the outlet stream, from where you can tackle pt 636m to the north-east, but reached by a prudent initial climb east to avoid cliffs to the north. Point 636m is an unassuming summit, but the views towards and across Eagles Lough make the ascent worth while. It also provides a good viewpoint to evaluate route 33 if you had it in mind for another day.

From pt 636m head initially north for a few hundred metres, swinging left when steep ground permits, and so reach the rocky floor of that part of the corrie just to the north of Lough Coomanassig. Cross the corrie floor and from here tackle Knocknagantee to the south, a steep climb, but simple navigationally, with cliffs all the way on your left.

Knocknagantee (676m, 2.5 hours) has a substantial cairn perched close to cliffs to the east. It commands good views south and west, there being no higher mountain in either direction. You will also note a vast expanse of moorland reaching north to Knockmoyle, to which moorland we must now turn our attention.

Head west with a touch of north from the summit so crossing a stretch of this moorland. On this stretch, if you intend to cut the route short, look out for a track down on the left, the upper end of the track up which you laboured earlier, because this is the way you will return. For the moment however the target is pt 628m, over 1km away to the west of Knocknagantee and a point of no significance except for, and this makes it well worthwhile, the magnificent views it offers of the deep trough of Coomavoher (route 29) to the north.

Point 628m also means decision time. The lack of distinct features from here makes navigation difficult. The terrain is also much tougher: many short but tiring ascents and descents through slabs and crags, around lochans and over streams and swamps ..... but well worth the effort!

Just south of pt 628m, cross a fence and you will immediately plunge into this terrain. It's impossible to describe a route in detail: a few metres in either direction presents different obstacles to be overcome. Just keep doggedly on, aiming for the two small unnamed lakes just to the east of Coomavanniha Lough, itself a useful landmark because of the two prominent peninsulas on its eastern side and because it's by far the largest lake in the area.

You can head for home east from these two lakes, but in good visibility I suggest you climb through somewhat easier terrain to the plateau over 1km away, whose indistinct highs are marked as pts 578m and 552m on the map. About here you must find a rocky east-running spur, with cliffs and steep ground to north and south. At the base of the spur, look to the right where great, intimidating layers of cliff block any hope of a descent. Just as well you are where you are!

As you walk downhill along the spur watch out for a tongue of forest in the valley on your left. The left end of this is the next target and you can choose any convenient point to veer off the spur and cross the intervening bogland to reach it. Before you do so however, you have a stream to cross, though normally it shouldn't present any great difficulty. Once across, walk downstream through some rough, tussocky country to meet a track near the initial (and only) farmstead of the route. Take it past one dwelling on the left and then turn right to cross the bridge and reach the start.

ROUTE 35: COOMALOUGHA LOUGH

Extensive bogland to start and finish but it's well worth the soggy slog. You will long remember the first sight from close at hand of the great cliffs surmounted by rocky towers to the south-west of Lough Reagh and the climb along a narrow ramp to the splendid, rugged, rocky country around Coomalougha Lough. This route gives an alternative start for route 33.

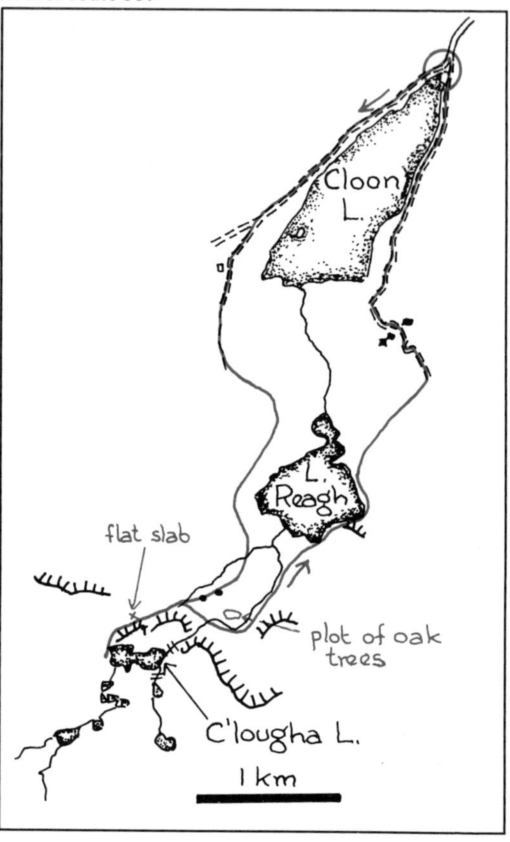

Getting There: The starting point (GR 709789) is at the same point as route 33.

Walking Time: 4.5 hours (distance 12km, climb 420m). In theory, this should take a modest 3.75 hours. The extra time is to allow for navigation and difficult terrain (some too vertical, some too horizontal - and therefore wet). Note that this does not include time for wandering around the lakes to the south of Coomalougha Lough, which could take at least 1.5 hours to explore.

Difficulties: Some attention to navigation is required for most of the route, though none of it is dreadfully difficult. The ascent to Coomalougha Lough looks impossible at first glance, and it certainly is steep but not life-threatening (this is not intended as an alarming reassurance).

Map: Sheet 78.

Route: Take the track on the right of the lake, fork left at the first junction, pass a derelict house and continue on the track and the subsequent path as it gradually becomes little better than notional.

The plan here is to walk along the western shore of Lough Reagh. The ground near the lough is soggy, but if you keep high (at about the 100m contour) you will cross several rocky promontories partly submerged in the bog and so reach a point just south-west of the lake comparatively unscathed (1).

Well before this point you will have become fully aware of the cliffs to the south-west of Lough Reagh. Impressive? .... let's just say that if they don't impress you, nothing will. In the centre of all this splendour is a short, grassy, twin-peaked spur, dwarfed by the cliffs behind. Walk to it and climb along its crest, noting the dense plot of oak trees (not easily confused with one of the several irregular scatterings hereabouts) growing at an extraordinary angle on the left of the spur, a reassurance that your navigation is correct. (You can walk to the right of this spur if you wish - the recommended route has the advantage of a clear landmark.)

Walk to the far (west) end of the spur, cross (maybe with difficulty) a narrow but deeply-set stream and start to walk uphill with a steeply rising but wide gully ahead. It divides a little way up; here take the right branch, thus passing a table-like slab, another useful reassurance.

The rest is easy, easy to describe anyway. Keep cliffs close on the left and climb, a tough walk but in a landscape that is nothing short of magnificent. After clambering through a tiny gap between rocks, take the steep but short drop to the western end of Coomalougha Lough where, surrounded by soaring crags, mighty expanses of slab and a lovely lake you will no doubt agree that all your efforts were worth while.

Give yourself plenty of time to explore the area of lakes to the south. If you walk clockwise round Coomalougha Lough you will probably find your way barred by crags on the shore just past the outlet stream from the lough. I waded round but maybe you can scramble over them.

The initial stage of the route back is the same as the outward journey but still take care with your navigation. Walk back to the western end of Coomalougha Lough. Here take a compass bearing of 30° to climb with mighty slabs on the right and so reach the tiny gap. Descend steeply to the grassy spur walked on the ascent.

For a change of scene you can keep the grassy spur high on your left and so descend into a narrow valley, the vertically-challenged clump of oaks now above you. Make your way initially east down the valley, crossing several streams as you go so that they are all eventually on the left.

Follow the main stream to near the southern shore of Lough Reagh and here veer right to walk the eastern shore. After you negotiate easy crags near the shore, watch out beyond them for a pebbly beach. Leave the lakeshore about here and, to avoid fences, head north with a touch of east over bogland to reach a shed a little above you and to the right of a cluster of houses. Take the track from here down to the houses and thence along the eastern shore of Cloon Lough to the start.

Note

(1) An earlier writer (Richard Mersey) describes wading through this area waist-deep in water. I don't understand how this could be, since the ground here is no wetter than many parts of my native Wicklow - that is soft and moist but not requiring swimming gear.

ROUTE 36: BOLUS HEAD

Much track and minor road parallel to the coast followed by an easy upland walk over Bolus Head giving good views seaward to the spectacular Skelligs.

Getting There: Start in the village of Ballinskelligs (GR 4365).

Walking Time: 3.75 hours (distance 13km, climb 530m), assuming a start at the youth hostel.

Difficulties: None.

Map: Sheet 83.

Route: From the youth hostel walk to the pier (it may of course be more convenient to start here). Walk the side road here marked 'no through road' and the lane beyond to its end. Cross a short stretch of beach and pick up the lane again on the far side. Where it ends turn left onto tarmac.

From here on simply follow the coastal road, an undulating progress with the sea below on the left and rough grazing mountainside on the right. On the way you will pass the pre-famine village of Cill Rialaig (now restored) among several forlorn reminders of abandoned settlements. Passing through the yard of the last farm on the tarred road the signal tower is a short distance away. It commands magnificent views of the Skelligs and the bird sanctuary of Puffin Island on its right.

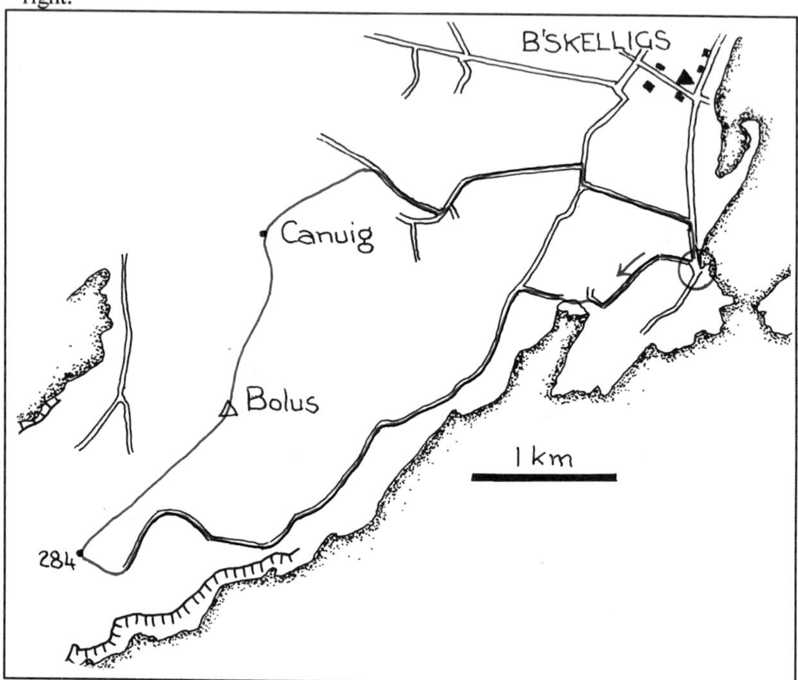

The return is along the modest tops. There is no clear path but the way is obvious. After Bolus Head (411m) itself you can climb the somewhat lower Canuig Mountain and then head towards the village, which lies to the east. Exactly what route you take depends on yourself: there is a network of roads (as shown on the sketch map) and therefore a plenitude of feasible routes.